W9-CGW-925

Snack Food

Sharon Dalgleish

Smart Apple Media

This edition first published in 2006 in the United States of America by Smart Apple Media.

Smart Apple Media
2140 Howard Drive West
North Mankato
Minnesota 56003

First published in 2006 by
MACMILLAN EDUCATION AUSTRALIA PTY LTD
627 Chapel Street, South Yarra, Australia 3141

Visit our Web site at www.macmillan.com.au

Associated companies and representatives throughout the world.

Library of Congress Cataloging-in-Publication Data

Dalgleish, Sharon.
  Snack food / by Sharon Dalgleish.
    p. cm. – (Healthy choices)
  Includes index.
  ISBN-13: 978-1-58340-748-6
  1. Nutrition—Juvenile literature. 2. Snack foods—Juvenile literature.
  3. Quick and easy cookery—Juvenile literature. I. Title.

RA784.D343 2006
641.5'39--dc22
                                          2005057578

Edited by Helen Bethune Moore
Text and cover design by Christine Deering
Page layout by Domenic Lauricella
Photo research by Legend Images
Illustrations by Paul Konye

Printed in USA

Acknowledgments
The author and the publisher are grateful to the following for permission to reproduce copyright material:

Front cover: Children sharing snacks, courtesy of Beth Field/Lochman Transparencies.

Brand X Pictures, p. 12; Corbis Digital Stock, p. 10 (left); Getty Images/Foodpix, p. 17; Getty Images/White Cross Productions, p. 8; iStockphoto.com, p. 4 (left); MEA Photo, pp. 1, 3, 10 (right), 23 (both), 26; Photodisc, pp. 11, 13, 16, 27; Photolibrary, p. 22; Photolibrary/Foodpix, p. 9; Photolibrary/Photonica Inc, p. 7; Photolibrary/Plainpicture Gmbh & Co. Kg, pp. 4 (centre), 30; Photolibrary/Reso E.E.I.G, p. 4 (right).

Contents

Healthy, fit, and happy

To be healthy, fit, and happy your body needs:

- a good mix of foods
- plenty of clean drinking water
- a **balance** of activity and rest

water

activity

A good mix of
foods, water, rest,
and play all help to
make you healthy.

mix of foods

Snack food

The food group pyramid can help you make healthy choices when you feel like a snack.

grains vegetables fruits oils dairy foods meat and beans

The food group pyramid shows you which foods to eat most for a healthy, balanced diet.

Why make healthy choices?

Making healthy snack food choices is important. Your stomach can **digest** only small amounts of food at a time. You need three main meals and two to three snacks a day.

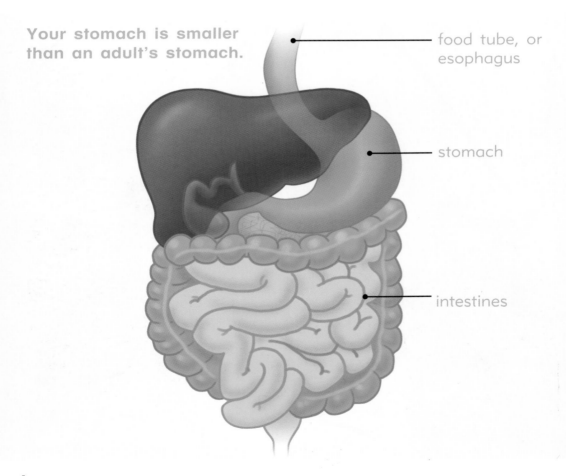

Your stomach is smaller than an adult's stomach.

food tube, or esophagus

stomach

intestines

A good snack is one that will give you **energy** now.
A healthy snack also gives you **nutrients** for later
so you keep well and grow strong.

You need lots of energy from food for all the things you do.

Fruit

Fruit is tasty, quick, and easy to prepare. When you are tired and hungry, you need a snack fast. That is a good time to reach for a piece of fruit.

An orange will give you quick energy for now as well as nutrients for later.

8

Different fruits contain different **vitamins**. All fruits are good for you in different ways. It does not matter which fruit you grab for a snack.

Try fruit dipped in low-fat yogurt.

Make banana sticks

Ask a parent or teacher for help.

Make these snacks-on-a-stick the day before you want to eat them.

Serves 2

What you need

- 1 banana
- honey, in a shallow dish
- dried or dehydrated coconut, in a shallow dish
- a knife
- 2 popsicle sticks
- tray lined with baking paper

What to do

1 **Peel the banana and cut it in half.**

2 **Push a popsicle stick into each half.**

3 **Roll each half in honey, and then in coconut.**

4 **Place the banana sticks on a tray lined with baking paper. Freeze overnight.**

Make watermelon cups

Ask a parent or teacher for help.

Serve these frozen fruit snacks with
a spoon on a hot day.

Serves 4

What you need

- seedless watermelon
- 4 small plastic cups
- a spoon
- a blender

What to do

1 **Cut the watermelon, then scoop out the flesh.**
2 **Puree in a blender until smooth.**
3 **Pour into small plastic cups.**
4 **Freeze overnight.**

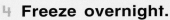

Vegetables

All vegetables are good for you, but it is best to avoid them if they are fried. French fries are not a good snack because they contain lots of fat.

Corn cobs can be grilled for a tasty snack.

If you have a garden, you can grow vegetables. Then you can pick a fresh snack whenever you need one. Fresh vegetables taste great and are full of vitamins!

Growing your own vegetables is a great way to have fresh snacks handy.

Make potato wedges

These homemade potato chips are baked, not fried, so they have less fat.

Serves 2 to 3

What you need

- 2 potatoes, peeled and cut into wedges
- olive oil spray
- pinch of salt
- a baking tray
- tongs
- oven heated to 450 °F (240 °C)

What to do

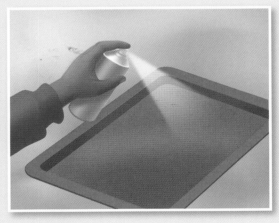

1 **Spray a large, shallow baking tray lightly with oil.**

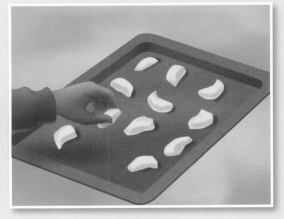

2 **Place potato wedges on the tray. Make sure they are in a single layer with none overlapping.**

Ask a parent or teacher for help.

3 Spray wedges lightly with oil, and sprinkle with a pinch of salt.

4 Bake in the oven for about 15 minutes. Turn over with tongs. Bake for another 15 minutes until brown and crisp.

Bread

Bread is filling and makes a healthy snack after school to keep up your energy. You can use bread in different ways to make all sorts of yummy snacks.

Have a snack before you do your homework to help you think clearly.

A toasted **savory** English muffin is a healthy snack after school or at any time. Add your favorite toppings and some cheese. Grill it to make your own pizza.

Toppings to try:

- ham, cheese, and tomato
- avocado and cheese
- pesto, chicken, and cheese
- tuna and cheese
- ham, creamed corn, and cheese
- baked beans, grated cheese.

Toasted sandwiches make a healthy snack, too.

Make egg-and-cheese rolls

These egg-and-cheese roll snacks can be eaten warm or cold.

Serves 1

What you need

- 1 round bread roll, with top sliced off
- 1 tablespoon grated cheese
- ½ cup chopped lean ham (if you like)

- 1 egg
- a small mixing bowl
- a fork
- a baking tray
- oven heated to 325 °F (160 °C)

What to do

1 **Dig out the inside of the roll. Place cheese inside the hole. Add ham if you like.**

2 **Break the egg into a small bowl and mix with a fork.**

Ask a parent or teacher for help.

3 Pour the egg into the roll.

4 Bake on a baking tray for about 25 minutes. The egg should be set and golden when you serve it.

Make French toast

Eat this toast as it is, or top with sliced banana.

Serves 1

What you need
- 1 egg
- 1 tablespoon milk
- 1 slice bread, cut in half
- 2 teaspoons butter
- a shallow bowl
- a fork
- a frying pan

What to do

1 **Break the egg into a shallow bowl. Add the milk and beat lightly with a fork.**

2 **Dip bread in egg mixture to coat each side.**

Ask a parent or teacher for help.

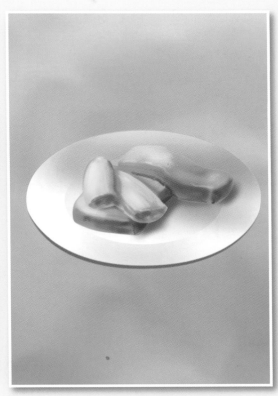

3 Melt butter in the frying pan
and place bread in pan.

4 Cook on both sides until
golden brown, and serve.

21

Sweet snacks

It is not a good idea to munch sugary treats every time a snack attack strikes. Sugar helps form a sticky coating, called plaque, on your teeth. Plaque causes teeth to rot.

A glass of water after a snack will help clean your teeth.

Make fruit balls

Ask a parent or teacher for help.

It is fine to have a sweet treat sometimes, especially if it is sweet and healthy.

Makes about 12 balls

What you need

- ½ cup dried apricots, chopped finely
- ½ cup dates, chopped finely
- ½ cup raisins
- 1 tablespoon condensed milk
- dried or dehydrated coconut
- a mixing bowl
- a wooden spoon
- a plate

What to do

1 **Mix apricots, dates, and raisins in a bowl. Add just enough condensed milk to make the mixture sticky.**

2 **Make balls by rolling teaspoons of the mixture between the palms of your hands.**

3 **Dip the balls in the coconut.**

4 **Place on plate and put in the fridge to set.**

Make oaty raisin bars

The wheat flour gives these sweet bars
extra **fiber**.

Makes about 24 bars

What you need

- ½ cup wheat self-raising flour
- 1 cup rolled oats
- 1 cup raisins
- ½ cup raw sugar
- ½ cup dried or dehydrated coconut
- 5½ ounces (155 grams) butter
- 1 tablespoon honey
- a mixing bowl
- a sieve
- a saucepan
- a rectangular tin
- a wooden spoon
- oven heated to 350 °F (180 °C)

What to do

1 **Sift flour into a large mixing bowl. Stir in the oats, raisins, sugar, and coconut.**

2 **Melt butter in the saucepan. Add the honey.**

3 **Pour butter and honey into the dry ingredients and mix well.**

4 **Press evenly into a well-greased rectangular tin. Bake for 15 to 20 minutes until golden. Cut into bars while hot. Remove from tin when cold.**

Snacks to pack

Most pre-packaged snacks contain a lot of sugar, fat, or salt, often called sodium. They do not have many nutrients to help you grow strong and stay well.

Healthy snacks should contain less than 120 milligrams of sodium, and less than 10 grams of fat per 100 grams.

Nutrition Facts

Serving Size ½ cup as packaged (27g)
½ cup prepared
Servings Per Container 5

Amount Per Serving	As pkgd	Prepared
Calories	90	130
Calories from Fat	10	35

	% Daily Value**	
Total Fat 1g*	2%	6%
Saturated Fat 0.5g	2%	6%
Trans Fat 0.5g		
Cholesterol 0mg	0%	1%
Sodium 590mg	25%	26%
Potassium 230mg	7%	8%
Total Carbohydrate 20g	7%	7%
Dietary Fiber 1g	6%	6%
Sugars 1g		
Protein 2g		

Vitamin A	0%	4%
Calcium	2%	6%
Iron	2%	2%
Riboflavin	0%	4%
Niacin	6%	6%

Not a significant source of vitamin C.

* Amount as packaged. As prepared, one serving provides 4g total fat (1g saturated fat, 1g trans fat), less than 5mg cholesterol, 630mg sodium, 280mg potassium, 22g total carbohydrate (3g sugars) and 3g protein.
** Percent Daily Values are based on a 2,000 calorie diet.

Plan your snacks ahead! You can pack snacks that are healthy and just as tasty as takeout. A hard-boiled egg makes a healthy snack and it is already wrapped.

Pack your own snacks when you go out.

Make popcorn

This popcorn has lots of flavor. There is no need to add butter or salt. For a sweet taste, add some chopped dried fruit and sunflower seeds when the popcorn is cooled.

Makes enough for 4 zip-lock bags

What you need

- ½ cup popping corn
- 1 tablespoon vegetable oil

- large saucepan with lid
- zip-lock bags

What to do

1 **Heat the oil on the stove in the saucepan and add the corn.**

2 **Put on the lid. Shake the saucepan to cover all the corn with oil.**

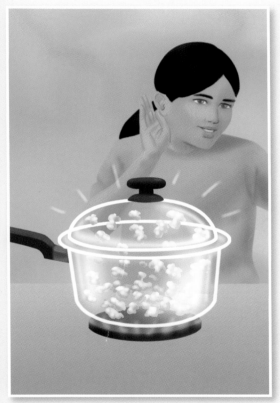

3 **Listen for the corn to start popping. Cook for about a minute until the popping stops.**

4 **Pack the popcorn in plastic zip-lock bags when it is cool.**

Healthy choices for life

Making healthy choices in everything you do will help you to be fit, happy, and healthy.

Life is fun when you make healthy choices.

Glossary

balance	an equal amount of different things
digest	to break down food and fluids inside the body
energy	strength to do things
fiber	found in plant foods, and helps your body break down food
nutrients	healthy substances found in food, such as vitamins and minerals
savory	tasty but not sweet
vitamins	healthy substances found in food

Index

THE MILITIA MOVEMENT

Other Books in the At Issue Series:

DISCARDED

THE MILITIA
MOVEMENT

David Bender, *Publisher*
Bruno Leone, *Executive Editor*

Scott Barbour, *Managing Editor*
Brenda Stalcup, *Series Editor*

Charles P. Cozic, *Book Editor*

AT ISSUE

An Opposing Viewpoints ® Series

Greenhaven Press, Inc.
San Diego, California

Library of Congress Cataloging-in-Publication Data

The militia movement / Charles P. Cozic, book editor.
     p.   cm. — (At issue)
  Includes bibliographical references and index.
  ISBN 1-56510-542-7 (lib. : alk. paper) — ISBN 1-56510-541-9 (pbk. : alk. paper)
    1. Militia movements—United States. 2. Government, Resistance to—United States. 3. Radicalism—United States. 4. Political violence—United States. I. Cozic, Charles P., 1957– . II. Series
HN90.R3M43   1997
322.4'2'0973—dc20   96-44910
                                                  CIP

©1997 by Greenhaven Press, Inc., PO Box 289009,
San Diego, CA 92198-9009

Printed in the U.S.A.

Table of Contents

Introduction

Militias in America date back to colonial times, when citizens agreed to provide their services and firearms for mutual defense. Today, militias consist of two types: government-sanctioned state militias and private citizen militias that are unaffiliated with government.

The citizen militia movement has grown rapidly during the 1990s, particularly in western states. Citizen militias in 1996 totaled 441 groups in fifty states, according to the Southern Poverty Law Center, a civil rights organization based in Montgomery, Alabama. These groups adhere to a variety of beliefs, from what many observers have called a paranoid distrust of government to endorsement of white supremacy to espousal of the right to own firearms. Law enforcement and other experts assert that, although widespread, militia members are well connected through computer networks, public forums, radio broadcasts, videos, and numerous publications.

Media and public attention toward citizen militias increased following several high-profile incidents. Militia members and other Americans argued that two federal raids against citizens that resulted in violence and death validated their warnings of an overly authoritarian government. In August 1992, federal law enforcement agents in Ruby Ridge, Idaho, surrounded the secluded cabin of Randy Weaver, wanted for illegal firearms sales. In a shoot-out, agents killed Weaver's wife and fourteen-year-old son and wounded Weaver and a friend. Near Waco, Texas, in April 1993, more than eighty members of David Koresh's Branch Davidian religious sect perished when a blaze destroyed their compound after federal agents invaded the complex to end a fifty-one-day siege. A total of five agents were killed by gunfire at Ruby Ridge and Waco.

Anger toward the government's role in these incidents led to much public support for citizen militias, experts contend. But these groups gained notoriety as well following the April 1995 bombing of an Oklahoma City federal building that killed 169 people. Law enforcement officials alleged that two suspects in the bombing, Timothy McVeigh and Terry Nichols, had attended militia meetings and may have received assistance and encouragement from militia members. At the same time, some militia groups theorized that the U.S. government itself orchestrated the blast in order to discredit the militia movement.

Many militia groups warn that Ruby Ridge and Waco are precursors to further abuses of power against private citizens by an oppressive federal government. In fact, Militia of Montana leader John Trochmann maintains that he created his group largely because of the events at Ruby Ridge and Waco. Trochmann and other militia leaders assert that citizen militias are the last line of defense protecting constitutional freedoms against a federal government that they believe is increasingly encroaching on personal rights, including property rights and the right to own firearms. According to Trochmann, "We view the militia movement as a giant neighborhood watch. America has nothing to fear from patriots maintaining 'vigilance.' She should, however, fear those that would 'outlaw' vigilance." John Parsons, who was the head of South Dakota's Tri-States Militia before it disbanded, takes a more combative stance:

> Here's our threat—that if there is a move to do away with our Constitution and Bill of Rights, or to move us into some fuzzy global world under the United Nations, we're going to fight and die with guns, bullets, and tanks and whatever we can get our hands on.

Fundamental to freedom and the protection of constitutional rights, militia members argue, is Americans' Second Amendment right to own firearms. They insist that the amendment's reference to "a well regulated Militia" applies to private citizen militias as well as to government militias. Northern Michigan Regional Militia leader Norman E. Olson writes, "The primary defense of the state rests with the citizen militia bearing its own arms."

Many critics, however, believe that the right to own firearms does not extend to citizen militias and that private militias are not protected under the U.S. Constitution. According to former U.S. Supreme Court justice Warren E. Burger, "In referring to 'a well regulated militia,' the [U.S. Constitution's] Framers clearly intended to secure the right to bear arms essentially for military purposes."

Furthermore, many opponents of militias contend that the militias' endorsement of violence justifies government efforts to suppress the groups. Just two months after the Oklahoma City blast, in June 1995, a U.S. Senate subcommittee held a hearing on citizen militias. Senator Carl Levin of Michigan testified that many militias pose a violent threat by stockpiling firearms and explosives. Levin added that self-described militia members have made threatening telephone calls to Bureau of Alcohol, Tobacco, and Firearms (BATF) agents, including the agency's director. James L. Brown, a BATF deputy director, told the subcommittee that some militia members had assaulted or shot at federal and local law enforcement personnel. According to Levin, "These instances seem to indicate an organized effort against law enforcement officials."

Critics also contend that the racist sentiment among some militia groups poses a threat to minorities. For example, at the June 1995 Senate hearings, Brown asserted that many militias either advocate white supremacy or are affiliated with white supremacist organizations. Indeed, Southern Poverty Law Center researcher Tawanda Shaw estimates that forty-five militias in twenty-two states have ties to white supremacists. Civil-rights organizations such as the Anti-Defamation League warn that some white supremacist groups may be participating in paramilitary training in preparation to commit violence against minorities.

According to New York congressman Peter T. King, such evidence is reason enough to crack down on "scores of heavily armed private armies . . . laced with xenophobic and racist elements." He writes,

> The citizen militia movement threatens the very fabric of a democratic society. Militia members who threaten government and law-enforcement officials with violence are dangerous and should be treated accordingly.

Militia opponents argue that strong measures are required to counter illegal militia activity. These include increased federal surveillance and the enforcement of laws in many states that prohibit unauthorized paramilitary training. In addition, Carl Levin argues, a federal statute outlawing paramilitary activities should be considered. And in 1995, according to *Newsweek* magazine, the FBI allegedly created a secret task force called the Executive Working Group on Domestic Terrorism, which has reportedly used electronic eavesdropping, undercover agents, and informants to monitor militia members.

However, many observers contend that while the government has a duty to protect the public against the threat of violence, it should be careful not to overreact against militias. Doing so, they argue, could make matters worse by fueling militia members' distrust and hatred of government. According to sociologist Brent L. Smith, author of *Terrorism in America*, it is important "not to demonize the demonizers. If Congress makes militias illegal, if they pass more gun control laws, we could see these groups grow in size and scope."

Supporters of citizen militias view the groups as necessary for the protection of constitutional rights. Opponents contend that militias threaten peace and democracy, no matter how patriotic their intentions. The authors in *At Issue: The Militia Movement* debate the goals and actions of militias and examine whether these groups constitute a danger to America.

1

Citizen Militias Defend Liberty

Norman Olson

Norman Olson is the commander of the Northern Michigan Regional Militia, which he cofounded in 1994. Olson, also a Baptist minister, testified before a U.S. Senate subcommittee hearing on militias in June 1995.

Armed citizen militias act as a rightful defense against external and internal threats to Americans' security and liberty. Militias—a manifestation of humans' instinctive desire to protect themselves—are purely defensive groups that devote themselves to civilian preparedness. The U.S. Constitution's Second Amendment provides a legal foundation for the existence of citizen militias. The natural right of the people to guard themselves against tyrannical government—mandated by the Declaration of Independence—cannot be denied.

Is the citizen militia legitimate and lawful in Michigan? The Governor, Lawmakers, and others say no. You've heard their lies. Now here are the facts.

The Second Amendment to the Constitution of the United States recognizes the inherent right of states to form militia units. That amendment reads:

> A well-regulated militia, being necessary to the security of a free State, the right of the people to keep and bear arms shall not be infringed.

Not only does the Constitution allow the formation of a Federal Army, it specifically recognizes state militias, and confirms that the citizen and his personal armaments are the foundation of the citizen militia. The arming of the militia is not left to the state but to the citizen. Should the state choose to arm its citizen militia, it is free to do so under the United States Constitution (bearing in mind that the Constitution is not a document limiting the citizen, but rather one that establishes and limits the power of government). Should the state fail to arm its citizen militia, the right of the people to keep and bear arms becomes the source of

Norman Olson, "Is the Citizen Militia Unlawful?" position paper of the Northern Michigan Regional Militia, 1995. Reprinted with permission.

the guarantee that the state will not be found defenseless in the presence of a threat to its security. *It makes no sense whatsoever to look to the Constitution of the United States or that of any state for permission to form a citizen militia.* Logic demands that the power to grant permission is also the power to deny permission. Brought to its logical conclusion in this case, a state may deny the citizen the right to form a militia. If this were to happen, the state would assert itself as the *principle* of the contract making the people the *agents*. Liberty then would be dependent on the state's grant of liberty. Such a concept is foreign to American thought. While the Second Amendment to the U.S. Constitution acknowledges the existence of state militias and recognizes their necessity for the security of a free state and while it also recognizes that the right of the people to keep and bear arms shall not be infringed, *the Second Amendment is not the source of the right to form a militia nor to keep and bear arms.* Those rights existed in the states prior to the formation of the federal union. In fact, the right to form militias and to keep and bear arms existed from antiquity. *The enumeration of those rights in the Constitution only underscores their natural occurrence and importance.* The Tenth Amendment to the U.S. Constitution reads:

> The Powers not delegated to the United States by the Constitution, nor prohibited by it to the States, are reserved to the States respectively, or to the people.

Power resides with the people

Ultimate power over the militia is not delegated to the United States by the Constitution nor to the states, but resides with the people. Consequently, the power of the militia remains in the hands of the people. Again, the fundamental function of the militia in society remains with the people. Therefore, the Second Amendment recognizes that the militia's existence and the security of the state rests ultimately in the people who volunteer their persons to constitute the militia and their arms to supply its firepower. The primary defense of the state rests with the citizen militia bearing its own arms. *Fundamentally, it is not the state that defends the people, but the people who defend the state.* The secondary defense of the state consists in the statutory organization known as the National Guard. Whereas the National Guard is solely the creation of statutory law, the militia derives its existence from the inherent inalienable rights of man which existed before the Constitution and whose importance are such that they merited specific recognition in that document. While the National Guard came into existence as a result of legislative activity, the militia existed before there was a nation or a constitutional form of government. The militia consisting of people owning and bearing personal weapons is the very authority out of which the United States Constitution grew. This point must be emphasized. Neither the citizen's militia nor the citizen's private arsenal can be an appropriate subject for federal legislation or regulation. *It was the armed militia of the American colonies whose own efforts ultimately led to the establishment of the United States of America!* While some say that the right to keep and bear arms is granted to Americans by the Constitution, just the opposite is true. The federal government itself is the child of the armed citizen. We the people are the parent of the child we call government. The increasing amount of federal encroachment into the territory of the Second Amendment in particular and the Bill of Rights in general indicates the need for parental corrective action. In short, the federal government needs a good spanking to make it behave.

One other important point needs to be made. Since the Constitution is the limiting document upon the government, the government cannot become greater than the granting power; that is, *the servant cannot become greater than his master.* Therefore, should the Chief Executive or other branch of government or all branches together act to suspend the Constitution under a rule of martial law, all power granted to government would be canceled and defer back to the granting power, the people. *Martial law shall not be possible in this country as long as the people recognize the Bill of Rights as inalienable.* The present actions of this country's government have been to convince Americans that the Bill of Rights controls the people. The Bill of Rights has nothing to do with control of the people, nor control of the government established by the people. The Bill of Rights stands as immutable and unaffected by any change determined upon the Constitution by government.

In Michigan, the militia is the subject of Article III, §4:

> The militia shall be organized, equipped and disciplined as provided by law.

The law alluded to speaks of militias of the state, to be equipped, supported and controlled by the Governor. A thoughtful consideration of this arrangement leads immediately to the question of *"Who really governs the militia?"*

Article I, §1 of Michigan's Constitution says,

> All political power is inherent in the people. Government is instituted for their equal benefit, security and protection.

Once again we see the inherent right of citizen militias vested in the people. The organizing and support of a state-sponsored militia of the state is a power granted to the Governor. This fact is further supported by Art. I, §7,

> The military shall in all cases and at all times be in strict subordination to the civil power.

But which military? It cannot be the citizen militia since the agent of a contract cannot control the principle. Therefore, the military spoken of is the military force permitted to be formed by the state, which is the National Guard. Neither can it be the citizen militia because, like the Federal Constitution, the Constitution of Michigan is the child of vested power reserved to the people forever. There is no possible way that the Governor of this State or the Chief Executive of the United States or any legislative body can "outlaw" the citizen's militia, for to do so would rob inherent power from the people and thereby transform the limited Constitutional Republic to a government-controlled state. If that were to happen, our entire form of government would cease.

Citizen militias are natural entities

How, then, can the citizen militia be controlled? It cannot be. It is the natural occurrence of the people. Historically, citizen militias emerge when a clear and present danger exists, threatening the well-being of the people. It would stand to reason that power granted to the Governor to form a militia for the security of the people is intended to reduce the need for the citizen militia. Simply, if the National Guard did its job in securing the state, the citizen militia would not emerge. That it has emerged so dramatically seems to indicate that the people do not feel secure. Nor can the people be given promises of security. Well-being is not measured by promise, but by experience. Surely our experience has been that security is lacking, hence the emergence of the citizen militia. When safety and security are reestablished in Michigan, the citizen militia will return to its natural place, resident within the body of the people, only to emerge again when security is threatened. Security is the common desire of all mankind. We can no more control the militia than we can change the nature of men. For their safety and security, people everywhere will form militias if and when necessary.

The federal government needs a good spanking to make it behave.

By now it should be clear that the militia predates state and federal constitutions. Its right to exist among the citizenry cannot be subjected to legal challenge. The only effective challenge to citizen militias would be political engineering. One may envision an effort to amend both the state and federal constitutions, specifically abolishing the right for citizens to form militia units. Should such a venture be dared, the natural need of the citizen militia would increase, actually drawing more free people to it. By now also, one should draw the conclusion that the militia is inherent to all social, interactive people concerned about the well-being of fellow citizens. This conclusion is that which is so clearly stated in the Bill of Rights. No man-made law can abolish the citizen militia since such a law would be in fact an unlawful act designed to dissolve power vested in the people. Such an effort would reveal an intent of any tyrant to transform *limited government created by the people* into a *government limiting the people*. Most tyrants know that such a move must be well timed. It is no wonder, then, that power-hungry central government and groomed courts view the Second Amendment as applying only to organized militias; i.e., armies of the individual states, that is, the National Guard.

To summarize: Citizen militias in Michigan are historic lawful entities predating all federal and state constitutions. Such militias are "grandfathered" into the very system of government they created as clearly revealed in both the Constitution of the United States and that of Michigan. These constitutions grant no right to form militias, but merely recognize the existing natural right of all people to defend and protect themselves. The governments created out of well-armed and free people are to be constantly obedient to the people. Any attempt to take the means of freedom from the people is an act of rebellion against the people. Currently in Michigan, the citizen militia is subject only to the historic role of American militias as defined in Black's Law Dictionary:

> Militia: The body of citizens in a state, enrolled for discipline as a military force, but not engaged in actual service except in emer-

gencies, as distinguished from regular troops or a standing army.

In order to conform to this definition, and to remain able to oppose a rebellious and disobedient government, the citizen militia must not be connected in any way with that government lest the body politic lose its fearful countenance as the only sure threat to a government bent on converting free people into slaves.

Common questions

Now that you have a basis of fact and logic concerning the historic militia, we may proceed to commonly asked questions.

1. Explain why the U.S. Government should or should not allow the existence of the Militia.

The U.S. Government cannot allow or forbid the militia. The power to permit is the power to forbid. Since the militia is a natural response to fear in a societal context, any attempt to forbid the militia will logically cause the fear to grow, thereby increasing the size and the determination of the citizens to arm and protect themselves. Carried to its logical end, the restriction will result in an armed rebellion against the government.

2. Should the U.S. Government revise the Second Amendment so that it would be interpreted in one way and not according to the needs of extreme groups or individuals? Why/why not?

The Government cannot control the people—the people control the government. The government cannot revise the Second Amendment since the Federalist Papers clearly show that a state may arm itself against the federal army, which is the greatest threat to freedom. In our country, the federal army has stood far beyond its purpose. Our founding fathers would be horrified at the thought of taking away the right of the people to collectively protect themselves against the government. But remember that the Second Amendment is not a granted right, but merely an "echoed" inalienable right which is recognized in the Constitution. Therefore, since it is inalienable, no revision can affect the natural right of people to defend themselves against tyrannical government.

3. Do you think the Militias have a right to exist? Please elaborate.

The question is faulty because the premise is illogical. The citizen militia is not a created thing, but rather an existing defensive force ever-existent in the body of the people. As far back as you wish to go, you will find people in a social community coming together to protect themselves, be it from wild animals, bandits, or government soldiers. To suggest that anyone can stop the emergence of a militia is to deny the very nature of human beings living together and sharing in a common defense.

4. Do you think that these Militias are a part of the unorganized state militia of 1792? Please comment.

The militias mentioned in the 1792 act are statutory militias created by a government, to be equipped and trained by that government. The civilian militia movement is NOT a part of that organization often called the "organized militia." The unorganized militia emerging today is not a part of any organized government body but rather an exercise of the "Fourth Branch" of government: We the People. There must be a clear distinction here. The Michigan Militia, for example, we formed by a common consent of 28 men who felt that they must share the duty of defense. Those 28 have grown to millions across America, but the original intent is the same: to defend ourselves against tyrannical and oppressive government.

It logically follows that if and when the tyrants and terrorists are suppressed, the militia of the people will disperse once again into the body of the people, only to emerge again when people feel the common threat.

5. *Do you think that these militias pose a threat to the U.S. Government and its citizens?*

The militia MUST pose a tremendous threat to tyrants and terrorists who hide within the government. They pose no threat whatsoever to the U.S. Government or the citizens since the militia is made up of the U.S. Government (We the People) and its citizens. You must remember that all citizens are naturally a part of the citizen militia. In fact, the Declaration of Independence states:

> But when a long Train of Abuses and Usurpations, pursuing invariably the same Object, evinces a Design to reduce them under absolute Despotism, it is their Right, it is their Duty, to throw off such Government, and to provide new Guards for their future Security.

One may ask, "Who" would have the power to "throw off such Government"? The citizen militia, of course. This means that the will and the might of the citizen militia IS the government made up of the citizens. The citizen militia, then, becomes the threat to a bad government system that will not change. The Declaration of Independence mandates that the citizen militia rise up in arms against *tyrants* and *despots*.

6. *Do you think these militias are there to protect the citizens from the abuses of government? Explain how.*

The citizen militia are the citizens protecting *themselves*. We cannot and will not protect people who refuse to protect themselves. The citizen militia *are* the citizens taking up arms in their own defense. You must break away from the *we v. them* mindset that the media and your professors have sold to you.

I urge you to set aside your intellectual traps and start thinking *logically*. Your questions give you away as someone who has taken the "pitch" of the fascists who want you to believe that the militias are in some way bad and dangerous. If you approach your argument from a logical human reasoning standpoint, you will find that militias are very natural and a very powerful dynamic in the history of the world.

Birth of the Northern Michigan Regional Militia

7. *What process did you use to establish the militia?*

While other organizations had gone "underground," I determined that visibility was essential to establish the legitimacy that we needed in the eyes of the public. We began with a huge media campaign. The first year (1994) was devoted to what we called "Operation Visibility." The media was exploited as a vehicle to carry the message of the Patriot Movement nationwide. I used the same methods that other popular front movements have used: extreme rhetoric and propaganda. But please remember that these methods are good and positive if they bring a heightened awareness of an immediate problem to the people. These are the same methods used by Patrick Henry and Tom Paine (who we often label as a bad guy).

The motivation was fear. But I must qualify that kind of fear with an explanation that fear is not a bad emotion, but rather a good emotion if it begins a process to bring safety to the one who is frightened. (The fear of fire will compel one to install fire alarms, for example.) Since the Waco incident and the Ruby Ridge killings [confrontations in which federal agents and private citizens were killed], the American people have grown increasingly frightened of their government. Others have grown fearful of the threat of the United Nations and the New World Order along with our loss of sovereignty as Americans. Some are frightened of law enforcement, others of the social services agents, still others of the IRS and the tax collectors, a few are even scared of the DNR [Department of Natural Resources] and the EPA [Environmental Protection Agency].

No man-made law can abolish the citizen militia since such a law would be in fact an unlawful act designed to dissolve power vested in the people.

Fear brings a response. There are three responses: 1) Fight, 2) Flight, 3) Denial. Some people are so frightened they deny the things that frighten them and find ways to rationalize. This often leads to "neurotic anxiety" and general paranoia. Others will face their fears, examine them, and go about doing something to reduce the fear. There are two ways of dealing with danger: 1) Fight, 2) Defend. Since we are a purely defensive movement, we have spent all our time in the business of defensive preparedness. But, since danger lurks everywhere, we must defend against all foreseen possibilities. For example, if economic collapse occurs, the enemy will be hunger and severe shortages. To maintain control (which is really the opposite of fear) we have spent time preparing food stores and other supplies to get us through a time of difficulty which seems to be growing more possible. So the answer is the being able to address the fears and to build a positive response to them.

8. How many people were initially part of the militia? And what about now?

The militia is made up of all able-bodied citizens not otherwise enlisted in the organized (federal/state) military.

9. What kinds of problems did your group run into, if any?

The chief problem we encountered was this: "If the perception of fear built the militia, and the militia taught people how to deal with the fear, what would happen if we helped people cease to be frightened?" That is precisely what we started out to accomplish. The problem was that the motivation, or fuel, which powered the engine, was going to run out if the engine did what it was supposed to do. In this case, there was no real problem. I determined that if the militia did its job, it would Arm, Equip, and Inform the American people. We would be prepared and ready for any attack on our sovereignty, or property, or our families. Now we are! We are ready and well able to defend ourselves against any tyrant from the local bureaucrats all the way to President Bill Clinton and [U.S. attorney general] Janet Reno. You see, the militia's rapid growth is directly proportional to the fear level in the people. But the militia has helped people deal directly with what has frightened them. Now that they can deal with it, they have courage. This courage has caused them to change from frightened Americans to watchful and cautious Americans. This has brought them confidence and has given them a sense of greater power. Now they will feel brave enough to stand up and to speak out about issues. This is what is happening. This has happened as I had planned. Essentially, I wanted to *work myself out of a job!!* That means, I want all Americans to be watchful since "the price of liberty is eternal vigilance."

If there is a problem, it is how to control what I call *"wing nuts."* These are people who have their own agenda and are generally fueled with bitterness and hatred and who feel that anarchy is the only way to achieve their ends. This includes people motivated against a race or religion. This is a general problem for all governments since the whole business of society is trying to maintain a balance between *tyranny* and *anarchy*.

10. What did you gain by forming the militia? What did you hope to gain?

The question could probably be stated better as "Did you achieve your goal?" The answer is YES. The people have been informed, trained, and equipped. There is a new level of awareness today. People everywhere are asking questions, holding elected officials to their oaths, getting involved, and demanding investigations into corruption and the abuse of power. This is good because it means that people are taking charge once again. We have tried to give America back to the people. It is the only way to avert civil war where the people rise up against the government. We have achieved our goals by redirecting the course of this nation. Now that millions of Americans are closely involved in government and are "watch dogging" it, I feel that IF civil war or economic collapse does come, many more people than before will be willing to resolve the problem and help establish a better government which will insure *life, liberty, and the pursuit of happiness*. We are seeing also the response by the Federal Government to "Angry Armed Americans." They have grown frightened of the people. There will be no more Wacos or Ruby Ridge events. And when the government fears the people, we will have liberty, but when the people fear the government, we will have tyranny.

As far back as you wish to go, you will find people in a social community coming together to protect themselves.

---

11. Do you think the militia is going in the direction you originally wanted it to?

Yes. The militia groups in America are networked and coordinated. Our leadership cadre is established and ready. We can muster more than a million soldiers within 24 hours who will help defend our country. We have commanders in all the states. The principles which were highlighted in our Militia Manual served to set the limits and bounds for our behavior. The Constitution and the Declaration of Independence will set the limit for our campaign. The Spiritual principles I have used will draw militia members to God and help them to remember that God still has a purpose for this country. Yes, we are on track. The bombing [of the Alfred P. Murrah Federal Building in 1995] in Oklahoma City set us back and we have only now been able to reform the troops, but now we are back and stronger and, I would hope, wiser than ever.

12. In the future, do you think the popularity of the militia will increase?

This cannot be foreseen. I believe that the Federal Government will continue its misinformation campaign against us. I believe that other government "events" will occur that will be blamed on the militia. But the American people are growing wiser by the day. They know that there is a cover-up of massive proportions concerning Waco, Whitewater [an Arkansas real estate and savings and loan affair investigated by Congress], Mena (the place in Arkansas where the CIA smuggled drugs into the U.S. under the watchful eye of Bill Clinton), and of course the present cover-up of the bombing in Oklahoma City. The people of America are growing smart! 1 hope they will be smart enough to see through any attempted covert action against the militias.

13. How do people view me?

Only history will judge that. We in America forget sometimes that men such as Samuel Adams, Patrick Henry, and even George Washington were hated and despised by many during the time of crisis. Remember that they were rebels who were essentially taking the law into their own hands. They were disobeying their legal government. They were involved in, or had knowledge of, the burning of customs houses and the sinking of customs vessels, the burning of British loyalist homes, the tarring and feathering of British agents. They threw tea overboard, broke up public meetings and gatherings, robbed government agents at gun point, and much more. Many people in their time felt they were vigilantes and bandits, but history has a way of washing off the dirt and looking at people somewhat more favorably. I would hope that history will be kind to me as well.

2

Militias Protect Against Authoritarian Government

Lyn Nofziger

Lyn Nofziger, a former presidential aide to Ronald Reagan, is a Republican political consultant and a novelist.

Militias consist of patriotic citizens dedicated to protecting liberty and resisting government intrusion into their lives. Such decent and law-abiding Americans correctly fear the possibility that government could take away their rights, including the right to own guns and to use their property as they choose. They also fear the advent of a one-world government. When the federal government oversteps its bounds, these Americans justifiably become angry and outraged. These citizens have every right to prepare to defend their freedom against government tyranny.

Editor's note: The following text originally appeared in Insight *magazine, where it was accompanied by an opposing article by Peter King, a Republican representative from New York.*

I am a wacko.
At least by Rep. Peter King's definition I am.
As such, I want to defend and make a case for many of my fellow right-wing wackos.

First, understand, we wackos do not trust government. We expect the worst from it. We believe there are many in it who distort the Constitution and seek to impose their will on a free people. We think such people endanger our liberty. We think, for example, that Bill Clinton is a bigger threat to our freedom than [Branch Davidian leader] David Koresh ever thought of being.

We wackos think there is a difference between legitimate laws and their proper enforcement on one hand and tyrannical laws and law enforcement run amok in such places as Waco and Ruby Ridge on the other.

We wackos believe the Fourth Amendment tells government to butt out of our lives unless it has just cause and that the Second Amendment guarantees us the right to protect ourselves—with guns, if necessary—

against tyranny and tyrants.

We wackos believe government is a necessary evil, not a necessary good. We believe small government is better and that government is best that governs least. Some of us even share Thomas Jefferson's belief that "the tree of liberty needs to be watered from time to time with the blood of patriots and tyrants."

These beliefs clearly set us apart from most of today's officeholders, for they represent a phenomenon of our times which, with rare exceptions, is that people elected for more than one or two terms come to believe they are smarter than the rest of us, know best what is good for us and have been ordained to rule us.

[Militia members] mean no harm; they are not a threat to freedom.

That is one reason why some people out in the countryside spend their weekends playing soldier. They mean no harm; they are not a threat to freedom. That threat comes from those in government who want to control the rest of us and intrude in our lives.

King believes those of us wackos who make up the citizen militias "threaten the very fabric of a democratic society." That belief puts him in a wacko class all his own. For, certainly, there are larger and more real threats to the fabric of our society than a few folks practicing at soldier because they fear the principles and motives of their national leaders.

You want threats to the fabric of society? Consider the breakup of the American family with its hordes of unmarried mothers, illegitimate children and deadbeat fathers. Consider the 14-year-old gun-toting gang members or the thousands of dope dealers. Consider the collapse of our education system or history's most expensive failure—the federal war on poverty.

Citizens preparing for the worst

Compare these to a few isolated groups of worried, frustrated men and women preparing for the American Armageddon. They don't bother me. Rep. King has to be paranoid for them to bother him. Some of us like the idea that still there are Americans who are not intimidated by those who want to sic the forces and resources of the federal government on anyone who dares to live and think outside the cultural, political and religious mainstreams of our society.

And, by the way, those militia bogeymen some fear so much really are out there on weekends, in the hills and mountains, in the forests, on the deserts. They are marching, training, disassembling and reassembling their hunting rifles (which Clinton says it's all right for them to have—at least for now), their carbines, their old World War II M1s and their shotguns.

During the week, like most law-abiding Americans, these people go about their businesses, running the gas stations, clerking in the hardware stores, preaching in the community churches, plowing the fields, going to war if their nation calls.

But even as they go about the business of everyday living, they also are preparing for the day the traitors in Washington and on Wall Street, the members of the Council on Foreign Relations, the Trilateralists and the Bilderbergers move to take over their country, move to establish a one-world dictatorship, move to take away the last of their liberties.

Maybe they are wrong but, by God, if it happens they are right, they are not going to sit idly by and let it happen. They will fight, if they must, as their forefathers fought at Bunker Hill to keep it from happening. Throughout the nation these little bands of men and women are determined that they will, as it says on New Hampshire's auto license plates, "Live Free or Die."

Hurray for them!

We are told by those who scoff at them, who fear them, who would outlaw them and take away their guns, that they are paranoid. That may be true, but it is always well to remember that even paranoids have enemies.

Furthermore, they are not alone. There also is another group of paranoids in our midst. Some occupy the White House and the Justice Department. Others sit in the Congress and the legislatures. Others clutter up the courts at every level and still more lurk within the media.

These are people who, with little logic, are fearful of men who, with real reason, are fearful of them. These are people who profess to believe in liberty but favor laws to limit and inhibit liberty. They reject any thought that men should prepare to fight to retain their liberty if it happens that it is their own government that seeks to take it.

There are millions more like [militia members], millions who are fed up with the way government intrudes more and more into their lives.

Indeed, these people cannot understand why rational men can and should fear their own government. They cannot believe that a government "conceived in liberty and dedicated to the proposition that all men are created equal" can become tyrannical or that they, however well-intentioned, are among those who would inflict tyranny upon the rest of us.

Rep. King is confused. He thinks that because he calls himself a conservative and has been twice elected to Congress that he has the right and duty to judge the motives, the sanity and the patriotism of others.

Like Clinton, he thinks one must love the government in order to love one's country. He forgets that the United States came into being on the heels of a revolution instigated and fought by men who rejected a tyrannical government and who were willing to die for freedom. Why should it be different today? Why should people accept oppression? Is liberty any less dear? Is government any more benign? Are those who seek to rule any more benevolent?

There are different ways to categorize Americans. One way is to separate those who love government from those who fear it. Another is to recognize that some Americans put security first while others put freedom first. A third is to identify those who believe citizens have no recourse except to obey all laws, no matter how questionable or ridiculous some might be.

Fortunately, there were men 220 years ago who, because they disagreed with that last premise, founded a nation that at least was conceived in liberty. In doing so they set a precedent that says freedom is and should remain America's most precious commodity, and that liberty remains worth fighting for.

Unfortunately, many in high places do not hold that belief. Instead, they adhere to a philosophy that says government knows best and must be obeyed and that they have been selected not to serve the people but to rule them.

The tip of the iceberg

King clearly does not understand those who reject that philosophy; does not realize that those people playing soldier are only the tip of the iceberg.

For, in fact, there are millions more like them, millions who are fed up with the way government intrudes more and more into their lives.

They may not want to play soldier. They may not own guns. But still, they fear the day is coming when they will have to choose between defending their rights as a free people or accepting a government that daily gnaws away at those rights.

The FBI, the U.S. Marshals Service and the ATF [Bureau of Alcohol, Tobacco, and Firearms] are the visible arms of those who would limit individual rights such as gun ownership and property use. And when these organizations step outside of their legitimate bounds, as they did at Ruby Ridge and Waco, Americans properly react in anger and outrage.

They know there is a vast difference between law officers who are doing their sworn duty and those who are abusing their fellow citizens. Yes, we need police officers. Yes, we need law and order. No one denies that. But, no, we do not need laws and law officers that trample on the rights of free people.

Yes, some Americans fear the advent of one-world government. Some Americans think big government and big business and big media are in a never-ending conspiracy to take away their rights and "keep them in their place." Some Americans think that when guns are outlawed only outlaws will have guns. But there are other Americans who want a one-world government, who would outlaw guns, who would make it illegal to play soldier and who would put under surveillance people or groups who don't conform or who interpret the Constitution or the Bible differently from you and me.

I like the idea of having those men and women out there in the woods, trained and ready to take on any conspirators.

And yes, some Americans are fearful that we have a government run by people who just might try to do such things. Those Americans—those wackos—even though they play soldier and prepare for the American Armageddon are, for the most part, decent, God-fearing, patriotic Americans. Their problem is that they don't like what they think is going on in this country and, because they are suspicious of government and authority, they figure there is a lot more going on that they would like even less if they knew what it was.

The main difference between most of them and the rest of us wackos is that they also believe a massive international conspiracy is to blame for what is wrong and what is going wrong. Of course that is not the case—I hope. Mostly, I don't think it is because I don't think any internationalist groups or any military-industrial combines are smart enough or tough enough to take over this country. Furthermore, I don't think Richard Nixon intended to and and I don't think Bill Clinton could get away with it, even with Hillary's help.

But just in case I'm wrong, I like the idea of having those men and women out there in the woods, trained and ready to take on any conspirators who might stick up their heads. I'd rather depend on them to defend my freedom than almost any member of Congress or the federal government that I can think of.

3

Militias Have a Constitutional Right to Own Guns

Daniel J. Schultz

Daniel J. Schultz, a U.S. Military Academy graduate, is a practicing attorney in Los Angeles and is the president and cofounder of the Lawyer's Second Amendment Society, a nationwide network of attorneys who support individuals' right to keep and bear arms.

The wording of the U.S. Constitution's Second Amendment gives citizen militias the rights to exist and to own guns. The Framers of the Constitution used the words "well regulated militia" not to indicate that the federal government should regulate the militia but rather to refer to the necessity of citizen militias to train and equip themselves in an orderly fashion. There is no evidence that the Framers defined the militia as being anything other than "the whole of the people." The Framers believed that armed citizens would act as a common defense and would pose no threat to fellow Americans.

Key Points:
- "Well Regulated" had a different meaning in the late 1700s.
- The Framers feared a government monopoly of armed force.
- The Bill of Rights is a fence around the government.
- To the Framers, the Militia is every able-bodied person.
- Well Regulated Militia = Self-Regulated Sharpshooters.
- The Armed Citizen is a force for civil peace.

The Second Amendment to the United States Constitution states: "A well regulated Militia, being necessary to the security of a free State, the right of the people to keep and bear arms, shall not be infringed." One of the terms used in the Second Amendment, the reference to the necessity of a "well regulated" militia, probably conjures up in most Americans today a connotation that is at odds with the meaning intended by the Framers' use of the term.

Daniel J. Schultz, "The 'Well-Regulated' Militia of the Second Amendment: An Examination of the Framers' Intentions," Firearms Sentinel, April 1995.

In today's English usage in America, the out-of-context use of the term "well regulated," in a constitution or a statute, at first blush, probably causes a vision of a *government* involved in heavy, intense regulation of the subject matter. However, as this viewpoint will show, that conclusion is wrong.

The words "well regulated" had a far different meaning when the Second Amendment was drafted. Moreover, the use of the term "well regulated"—both in the context of the Constitution's provisions for Congressional power over certain portions of the militia and in the context of the Framers' definition of "militia"—shows that government regulation was not the intended meaning. Rather, the term means only what it says, that the necessary militia be well regulated. It does not mean well regulated by the national government.

Whenever one attempts to understand the meaning of terms used in the Constitution, one must start with the words of the Constitution themselves. If the meaning is plain, that meaning controls.[1] To ascertain the meaning of the term "well regulated" as it is used in the Second Amendment, it is necessary to begin with the purpose of the Second Amendment itself.[2]

The Framers' worldview

The overriding consideration of the Framers in guaranteeing the right of the people to keep and bear arms was to implement a check on the standing army which the Constitution empowered the Congress to "raise and support."[3] As Noah Webster put it in a pamphlet urging ratification of the Constitution, "Before a standing army can rule, the people must be disarmed; as they are in almost every kingdom in Europe."[4]

George Mason remarked to his Virginia delegates regarding the colonies' recent experience with Britain, in which the monarch's goal had been "to disarm the people; that . . . was the best and most effectual way to enslave them."[5]

A widely reprinted article by Tench Coxe, an ally and correspondent of James Madison, described the Second Amendment's overriding goal as a check upon the national government's standing army:

> As civil rulers, not having their duty to the people duly before them, may attempt to tyrannize, and as the military forces which must be occasionally raised to defend our country, might pervert their power to the injury of their fellow citizens, the people are confirmed by the next article in their right to keep and bear *their private arms.*[6]

Thus, the well regulated militia necessary to the security of a free state was a militia that might someday fight against a standing army raised and supported by a tyrannical national government. That is the likely reason the Framers did not say "A Militia well regulated by the Congress, being necessary to the security of a free State." A militia so regulated might not be separate enough from, or free enough from, the national government, in the sense of both physical and operational control, to accomplish the goal of preserving the "security of a *free* State."

It is useful to review the general purpose of the Bill of Rights. To secure ratification of the Constitution, the Federalists urging passage of the

Constitution by the States, had committed themselves to the addition of the Bill of Rights, to serve as "further guards for *private* rights."[7] In that regard, the first ten amendments to the Constitution were designed to be a series of "shall nots," telling the new national government again, in no uncertain terms, where it could not tread.

It would be incongruous to suppose or to suggest that these amendments, including the Second Amendment—which were proscriptions on the powers of the national government—somehow simultaneously acted as a grant of power to the national government. With respect to the term "well regulated," it would make no sense to suggest that this referred to a grant of "regulation" power to the government, national or state, when the entire purpose of the Bill of Rights was to both declare individual rights and tell the national government, again, where the scope of its enumerated powers ended.[8]

The militia: the Framers' viewpoint

In keeping with the intent and purpose of the Bill of Rights both to declare individual rights and to proscribe the powers of the national government, the use and meaning of the term "Militia" in the Second Amendment, which needs to be "well regulated," helps us to ascertain what "well regulated" means. At the time of ratification of the Constitution, the Framers unanimously believed that the "militia" included all of the people capable of bearing arms.

George Mason, one of the Virginians who refused to sign the Constitution because of its lack of a Bill of Rights, said: "Who are the Militia? They consist now of the whole people."[9] Likewise, the *Federal Farmer*, one of the most important Anti-Federalist opponents of the Constitution, referred to a "militia, when properly formed, [as] in fact the people themselves."[10]

The list goes on and on. Nowhere is to be found a contemporaneous definition of the militia, by any of the Framers, that defines the militia as being anything other than the "whole body of the people." Indeed, as one commentator has said, the notion that the Framers intended the Second Amendment to protect the "collective" right of the states to maintain militias rather than the rights of individuals to keep and bear arms, "remains one of the most closely guarded secrets of the eighteenth century, for no known writing surviving from the period between 1787 and 1791 states such a thesis."[11]

> *To disarm the people . . . was the best and most effectual way to enslave them.*

Furthermore, returning to the text of the Second Amendment itself, the right to keep and bear arms is defined as a right retained by "the people," not the states. In 1990 the U.S. Supreme Court confirmed this view, finding that the right to keep and bear arms was an individual right held by the "people"—a "term of art employed in select parts of the Constitution," specifically the Preamble and the First, Second, Fourth, Ninth and Tenth Amendments.[12] Thus, the term "well regulated" ought to be considered in the context of the noun it modifies, the people themselves, the militia(s).

The above analysis leads us finally to the term "well regulated" itself, standing alone. What did these two words mean at the time of ratification? Were they commonly used to refer to a governmental bureaucracy as we know it today, with countless rules and regulations and inspectors, or something quite different?

We can begin this analysis by examining how the term "regulate" is used elsewhere in the Constitution. In every other instance where the term "regulate" is used, or regulations are referred to, the Constitution tells us who is doing the regulating and what is being "regulated."[13]

However, in the Second Amendment, the Framers chose only to use the term "well regulated" to describe a militia and chose not to define who or what would regulate the militia(s) to which they referred. It is important to note that the Framers' chose to use the indefinite article "a" to refer to the militia, rather than the definite article "the."

This choice suggests that the Framers were not referring to any particular well regulated militia but, instead, only to the concept that well regulated militias, made up of citizens bearing arms, were necessary to secure a free State. Thus, the Framers chose not explicitly to define who, or what, would be regulating the militias, nor what such regulation would consist of, nor how the regulation was to be accomplished.

The right to keep and bear arms is defined as a right retained by "the people," not the states.

Having compared the Framers' use of the term "well regulated" in the Second Amendment to the use of the words "regulate" and "regulation" elsewhere in the Constitution, we now return to an analysis of the meaning of the term in reference to its object, the militia. There is no doubt the Framers understood that the term militia included multiple concepts.

First, as we have seen, the Framers understood all of the people to be part of the unorganized militia.[14] These unorganized militia members, "the people," had the right to keep and bear arms. They could, individually, or in concert, well regulate themselves, that is, train to shoot accurately and to learn the basics of military tactics.

This interpretation is in keeping with English usage of the time, which included within the meaning of the verb "regulate" the concept of self-regulation or self-control (as it does still to this day).[15] The concept that the people retained the right to self-regulate their local militia groups (or regulate themselves as individual militia members) is in keeping with the Framers' choice of the indefinite article "a" in the term "A well regulated Militia."

The militia: one of the checks and balances

This concept of the people's self-regulation, that is, *non-governmental* regulation, is also in keeping with the limited grant of power to Congress "for calling forth" the militia for only certain, limited purposes,[16] to "provide for" the militia only certain limited control and equipment,[17] and the limited grant of power to the President regarding the militia, who only serves as Commander in Chief of that portion of the militia called into the actual service of the nation.[18] The "well regula[tion]" of the militia pronounced in the Second Amendment was apart from that exercise of control over the militia by Congress and the President, because that control only extended to that part of the militia called into actual service of the Union.

Thus, the "well regula[tion]" referred to something else. If we remind ourselves that the fundamental purpose of the militia was to serve as a check upon a standing army, it would seem the words "well regulated" referred to the necessity that the armed people making up the militia(s) be up to their primary task, that they have the level of equipment and training necessary to be a formidable check upon the national government's standing army.

This view is confirmed by Alexander Hamilton's observation, in *The Federalist, No. 29*, regarding the people's militia's ability to be a match for a standing army:

> . . . but if circumstances should at any time oblige the government to form an army of any magnitude, that army can never be formidable to the liberties of the people, while there is a large body of citizens, little if at all inferior to them in discipline and use of arms, who stand ready to defend their rights. . . .

It is a truism that law-abiding, armed citizens pose no threat to other law-abiding citizens. The Framers' writings show that they also believed this. As we have seen, the Framers understood that "well regulated" militias, that is, armed citizens, ready to form militias that would be well trained, self-regulated and disciplined, would pose no threat to their fellow citizens but would, indeed, help to "insure domestic Tranquility" and "provide for the common defence."[19]

Notes

1. In constitutional or statutory construction, language should always be accorded its plain meaning. *See, e.g., Martin v. Hunter's Lessee*, 14 U.S. (1 Wheat.) 304, 326 (1816).

2. "On every question of construction [of the Constitution] let us carry ourselves back to the time when the Constitution was adopted, recollect the spirit manifested in the debates, and instead of trying what meaning may be squeezed out of the text, or invented against it, conform to the probable one in which it was passed." Thomas Jefferson, letter to William Johnson, June 12, 1823, *The Complete Jefferson*, p. 32.

3. "The Congress shall have Power . . . To raise and support Armies. . . ." U.S. Const., Article I, Section 8, cl. 12.

4. Senate Subcommittee On The Constitution Of The Comm. On The Judiciary, 97th Cong., 2d Sess., The Right To Keep and Bear Arms (Comm. Print 1982), at 5.

5. 3 J. Elliot, Debates In The Several State Conventions 380 (2d ed. 1836).

6. Originally published under the pseudonym "A Pennsylvanian," these "Remarks on the First Part of the Amendments to the Federal Constitution" first appeared in the Philadelphia Federal Gazette, June 18, 1789, at

2, col. 1. They were reprinted by the New York Packet, June 23, 1789, at 2, cols. 1–2, and by the Boston Centennial, July 4, 1789, at 1, col. 2. The U.S. Supreme Court, in *U.S. v. Miller*, 307 U.S. 174, 83 L. Ed. 2d 1206, 59 S. Ct. 816 (1939), noted that the debates in the Constitutional Convention, the history and legislation of the colonies and states, and the writings of approved commentators showed that the militia comprised all males physically capable of acting in concert for the common defense—a body enrolled for military discipline.

7. 11 Papers Of James Madison 307 (R. Rutland & C. Hobson ed. 1977) (letter of Oct. 20, 1788, from Madison to Edmund Pendleton) (emphasis added).

8. An examination of the other nine amendments of the Bill of Rights shows that they were designed, like the Second Amendment, to declare rights retained by the people, or the States, and to provide a clear list of powers not given to the national government: "Congress shall make no law . . . ." (Amendment I); "No soldier shall . . . ." (Amendment III); "The right of the people . . . shall not be violated, and no warrants shall issue . . . ." (Amendment IV); "No person shall . . .; nor shall any person . . .; nor shall private property be taken . . . ." (Amendment V); "In all criminal prosecutions, the accused shall enjoy . . . ." (Amendment VI); "In Suits at common law . . . the right of trial by jury shall be preserved, and no fact tried by jury, shall be otherwise re-examined in any Court of the United States . . . ." (Amendment VII); "Excessive bail shall not be required . . . ." (Amendment VIII); "The enumeration in the Constitution, of certain rights, shall not be construed to deny or disparage others retained by the people." (Amendment IX); "The Powers not delegated to the United States by the Constitution, nor prohibited by it to the States, are reserved to the States respectively, or to the people." (Amendment X).

9. 3 J. Elliot, Debates In The General State Conventions 425 (3d ed. 1937) (statement of George Mason, June 14, 1788), reprinted in Levinson, *The Embarrassing Second Amendment*, 99 Yale L. Rev. 637, 647 (1989). *See supra* note 6 and accompanying text.

10. Letters From The Federal Farmer To The Republican 123 (W. Bennet ed. 1978) (ascribed to Richard Henry Lee), *reprinted in* Levinson, *supra* note 9, at 647. *See supra* note 6 and accompanying text.

11. S. Halbrook, That Every Man Be Armed: *The Evolution of a Constitutional Right*, p. 83 (The Independent Institute, 1984).

12. *U.S. v. Verdugo-Urquidez*, 494 U.S. 259, 265 (1990) ("The Second Amendment protects 'the right of the people to keep and bear Arms'. . . .").

13. "The Times, Places and Manner of holding Elections for Senators and Representatives, shall be prescribed in each State by the Legislature thereof; but the Congress may at any time by Law make or alter such Regulations, except as to the Places of chusing Senators." (Article I, Section 4); "The Congress shall have power . . . To regulate Commerce with foreign Nations, and among the several States, and with the Indian Tribes . . . ." (Article I, Section 8, cl. 3); "The Congress shall have power . . . To coin Money, regulate the Value thereof, and of foreign Coin, and fix the Standard of Weights and Measures . . . ." (Article I, Section 8, cl. 5); "No Preference shall be given by any Regulation of Commerce or Revenue to the Ports of one State over those of another: nor shall Vessels

bound to, or from, one State, be obliged to enter, clear, or pay Duties in another." (Article I, Section 9); "In all Cases affecting Ambassadors, other public Ministers and Consuls, and those in which a State shall be Party, the supreme Court shall have original Jurisdiction. In all the other Cases before mentioned, the supreme Court shall have appellate Jurisdiction, both as to Law and Fact, with such Exceptions, and under such Regulations as the Congress shall make." (Article III, Section 2, cl. 2); "No Person held to Service or Labour in one State, under the Laws thereof, escaping into another, shall, in Consequence of any Law or Regulation therein, be discharged from such Service or Labour, but shall be delivered up on Claim of the Party to whom such Service or Labour may be due." (Article IV, Section 2, cl. 3); "The Congress shall have Power to dispose of and make all needful Rules and Regulations respecting the Territory or other Property belonging to the United States; and nothing in this Constitution shall be so construed as to Prejudice any Claims of the United States, or of any particular state." (Article IV, Section 3, cl. 2).

14. *See supra*, notes 6, 9 and 10 and accompanying text.

15. The Oxford English Dictionary gives the following examples of usage for the term "well regulated": 1709: "If a liberal Education has formed in us . . . well-regulated Appetites, and worthy Inclinations." 1714: "The practice of all well regulated courts of justice in the world." 1812: "The equation of time . . . is the adjustment of the difference of time, as shown by a well-regulated clock and a true sun dial." 1848: "A remissness for which I am sure every well-regulated person will blame the Major." 1862: "It appeared to her well-regulated mind, like a clandestine proceeding." 1894: "The newspaper, a never wanting adjunct to every well-regulated American embryo city."

One definition of the word "well" in the Oxford English Dictionary is "satisfactorily in respect of conduct or action."

One of the Oxford English Dictionary definitions for the term "regulated" is "b. Of troops: Properly disciplined." The one example of usage is: "1690: *Lond. Gaz.* No. 2568/3 'We hear likewise that the French are in a great Allarm in Dauphine and Bresse, not having at present 1500 Men of regulated Troops on that side.'" The Oxford English Dictionary, Second Edition (Clarendon Press, Oxford, 1989).

16. "The Congress shall have Power . . . To provide for calling forth the Militia to execute the Laws of the Union, suppress Insurrections and repel Invasions . . . ." U.S. Const., Article I, Section 8, cl. 15.

17. "The Congress shall have Power . . . To provide for organizing, arming, and disciplining the Militia, and for governing such Part of them as may be employed in the Service of the United States, reserving to the states respectively, the Appointment of the Officers, and the Authority of training the Militia according to the discipline prescribed by Congress . . . ." U.S. Const., Article I, Section 8, cl. 16.

18. "The President shall be Commander in Chief of the Army and Navy of the United States, and of the militia of the several States, when called into the actual service of the United States . . . ." U.S. Const., Article II, Section 2, cl. 1.

19. U.S. Const., Preamble.

4

Militias Can Achieve Their Goals Through Peaceful Means

William F. Jasper

William F. Jasper is the senior editor of the New American, *a biweekly publication of the conservative John Birch Society.*

Critics of the militia movement have portrayed militia members as menacing extremists and have distorted the meaning of the Second Amendment by claiming that there is no individual right to own guns. But a U.S. Senate subcommittee, after extensive legal research, concluded in 1982 that the individual citizen has a right to own and carry guns "in a peaceful manner." That there are some sinister elements within the militia movement—including racists and fascists—cannot be ignored. However, in order to gain legitimacy, militias should remove these negative elements and should stress civic responsibility. Militias that advocate armed resistance against the government merely hurt their own public image. Instead, they should preserve their rights through peaceful means.

The Establishment media cartel has discovered a new demon. Phil Donahue, Tom Brokaw, CNN, *Time* magazine, the *New York Times*, the *Christian Science Monitor*, the *Chicago Tribune*, and other politically correct paragons of the fourth estate have been reporting breathlessly on a dangerous and growing threat to the republic: Armed Militias.

In a December 12, 1994, article that is fairly typical of coverage nationwide, the *Philadelphia Daily News* presented militia members as paranoid gun nuts who "believe their government is brutally out of control, unlawfully seeking to seize their firearms." And, said the *Daily News*, they are convinced that "the only way for patriots to protect themselves against this tyranny is to pick up their guns—preferably assault rifles—and learn how to shoot Marines."

William F. Jasper, "The Rise of Citizen Militias," *New American*, February 6, 1995. Reprinted with permission.

Media misperception

The article by *Philadelphia Daily News* staff writer Don Russell presented a decidedly alarming picture of heavily armed bigots and kooks run amok:

> The way some from this growing fringe see it, it's an evil, totalitarian New World Order out there, full of lying politicians, UFOs, greedy international corporations, secretive government agencies, Zionist bankers, gun-grabbing liberals, foreign troops on American soil, mysterious supermarket bar codes and dizzying conspiracies.

> Under other circumstances, it might be easy to write this off as paranoid, bigoted cult lunacy. Some militia leaders have past connections with the KKK, Aryan Nation, Posse Comitatus and other white supremacist groups.

Russell quotes Barry Morrison, regional director of the Anti-Defamation League of B'nai B'rith in Philadelphia, as saying that the militia movement is "reflective of the thinking of right-wing extremists with apocalyptic fantasies. They're motivated under the umbrella of extreme religious views. They believe the forces of good shall wrestle with the forces of evil, and there will be an armed confrontation."

The vast majority of individuals involved in militia organizations do not remotely resemble . . . menacing villains.

You get the picture: rabid, right-wing, religious extremists with guns, swastikas, hoods, and burning crosses. But, hey, don't accuse the media "liberals" of stereotype overkill; they know how to provide "balance" in reporting. They'll grant that not *everybody* associated with the growing militia movement is a certified, goose-stepping Hitlerite. There are less menacing types as well: over-the-hill and over-weight bubbas living out Walter Mittyish "GI Joe" fantasies. The *Daily News'* Russell presents this "side" of the militia image in a companion piece entitled "Not exactly America's Finest." It begins:

> If citizen militias are the valiant patriots who are going to defend America from tyranny, God help us.

> Imagine 40 or 50 pot-bellied guys from the corner taproom wearing I. Goldberg surplus fatigues and Doc Marten boots, playing hide-and-seek on a snowy field.

> Now give them semiautomatic weapons, which they may or may not know how to use, and you have a training session of the Southern Michigan Regional Militia. . . .

Not exactly a flattering portrait, or one likely to comfort communities where militias may be forming. But the theme—"Nazi Terminators Hook up With the Gang That Couldn't Shoot Straight"—is one that has gotten a lot of media play, and is almost certain to be cranked up louder. In December 1994 *NBC Nightly News* featured a special segment on the militias. While militia members in camouflage fatigues ran through drills in the Michigan woods, NBC reporter Jim Cummins intoned, "This is the

Michigan Militia, a self-proclaimed fighting force of ordinary citizens preparing to defend themselves—against the federal government." The NBC report warned that "civil liberties organizations say hate groups have infiltrated at least eight civilian militias" and that "police fear a deranged person could get the wrong message from a [militia] computer screen and start killing people."

On December 27th, 1994, Phil Donahue weighed in with his contribution. He railed at and ridiculed the militia representatives (from Michigan, Ohio, and Montana) who were his "guests," cut them off (in typical Donahue fashion) when they tried to answer his questions, and rolled his eyes and shook his head at their responses. "I still don't know what the hell you're doing in these funny outfits here," he mocked, referring to the militia uniforms (in which producers had asked them to appear). "What are you concerned about, gentlemen? What's going to happen? You think that the Feds are coming, they're going to suspend the Constitution, they're going to take your guns away. And you're practicing and when they come you're going to POP them. . . . Our government wants to disarm citizens, create a one-world government—C'MON!"

"Expert" analysis

Featured prominently in virtually every militia story are the "experts" and publications of the Anti-Defamation League of B'nai B'rith (ADL) and the Southern Poverty Law Center (SPLC). In November 1994, the ADL released *Armed and Dangerous: Militias Take Aim at the Federal Government*, a state-by-state report on the 13 states where the ADL says militia "extremists, numbering in the thousands," are preparing for "paramilitary resistance against the federal government." Many of these "embrace conspiracy fantasies involving the Council on Foreign Relations, the Trilateral Commission, and the Rockefeller Foundation," and advocate "the abolition of the Federal Reserve." Accordingly, the ADL report offers an "ADL Model Paramilitary Training Statute" to curb the dangers which it sees in the militias and says, "In states where such laws have yet to be adopted, ADL urges that they be given prompt consideration."

The Southern Poverty Law Center, headquartered in Montgomery, Alabama, is the creature of millionaire lawyer-activist Morris Dees, a financier of the George McGovern and Jimmy Carter campaigns and an implacable gun foe who boasted back in 1976, "Within five years we'll break the NRA [National Rifle Association]." Klanwatch, a project of SPLC, publishes the *Klanwatch Intelligence Report*. The cover story headline in the December 1994 issue of the newsletter loudly blared, "Racist Extremists Exploit Nationwide Militia Movement: White Supremacists Linked to Brigades in Nine States." Klanwatch Director Danny Welch was quoted in the story as saying, "The foot soldiers in these [militia] groups are just the type of people that Klan and neo-Nazi leaders have recruited in recent years. . . . This is one of the most significant and, potentially, most dangerous developments in the white supremacy movement in a decade." In a box on the same front page, Klanwatch announced that in October 1994 it had formed "a militia task force to systematically monitor hate group activity within the movement" and that, "beginning in February, 1995, the *Klanwatch Intelligence Report* will feature a special section called 'Militia Update.'"

On November 1, 1994, Morris Dees sent a letter on SPLC stationery to Attorney General Janet Reno urging her "to alert all federal law enforcement authorities to the growing danger posed by the unauthorized militias that have recently sprung up in at least eighteen states." Dees also sent a copy of the Reno letter, along with a fund-raising letter, to his supporters, appealing for funds so that the center might "monitor the activities of the new militias."

Thomas Jefferson: "[N]o free man shall ever be debarred the use of arms."

Dees and his race-baiting colleagues over at ADL know that this is the stuff that brings in big money from their liberal constituents and starts their fellow ideologues in the media salivating.

On the other hand, conservatives familiar with the ADL's and SPLC's penchants for seeing a fascist Klansman under every bedsheet may tend to reject *en toto* these groups' warnings as simply more of the smear jobs for which they have become notorious.

However, our own research—which includes interviews with dozens of militia leaders, members, sympathizers, and observers in 15 states—indicates that the ADL/SPLC/media alarms are not completely without basis. Although our investigation leads us to believe that the vast majority of individuals involved in militia organizations do not remotely resemble either the menacing villains or the pathetic misfits portrayed by the media and the militia critics, those elements do indeed exist. In fact, we found that it is often the militia leaders themselves who are most acutely aware of this problem, and who are working conscientiously to weed out the real extremists, racists, and hate-mongers.

Before looking at that issue in more detail, however, we must make a detour through another matter. Besides labeling the militia movement as racist-fascist, the critics have also muddied the waters with a confusing welter of misinformation about the legal, historical, and constitutional standing and meaning of the Second Amendment of the Bill of Rights as it relates to the militia and to the right of individuals to possess firearms. That amendment states:

> A well regulated Militia, being necessary to the security of a free State, the right of the people to keep and bear Arms, shall not be infringed.

News reports concerning the militia seem invariably to defer to the conventional "liberal" interpretation on this important constitutional matter, to wit: a) the amendment has to do with a "collective" right to bear arms, not an "individual" right; b) the collective right belongs to the militia, which is the National Guard; c) ergo, individuals and militias other than the National Guard have no right to keep and bear arms, and their stubborn insistence on this right is a threat to the "rule of law" and established order; and d) the views of the Founding Fathers, the courts, and the vast preponderance of legal scholars all support this view.

All of the above propositions are patently false, but they have been repeated so often, and have been so cleverly supported with sophisticated-sounding legal arguments, that they are widely believed.

"Except for lawful police and military purposes," says the American Civil Liberties Union, "the possession of weapons by individuals is not constitutionally protected." Following in the same vein, the ACLU of Southern California has held:

> Most scholars overwhelmingly concur that the Second Amendment was never intended to guarantee gun ownership rights for individual personal use. Small arms ownership was common when the Bill of Rights was adopted, with many people owning single shot firearms for hunting in what was then an overwhelmingly rural nation.

According to the Association of the Bar of the City of New York, the proposition "that the framers were concerned with the right of individuals to protect their homes and persons from whatever depredations might confront them, appears to be without historical support."

Attorney Roy G. Weatherup, in an oft-cited article in the *Hastings Constitutional Law Quarterly* (Winter 1975), writes: "In the last angry decades of the twentieth century, members of rifle clubs, paramilitary groups and other misguided patriots continue to oppose legislative control of handguns and rifles. These ideological heirs of the vigilantes of the bygone western frontier era still maintain that the Second Amendment guarantees them a personal right to 'keep and bear arms.'"

The Founding Fathers saw the militia . . . as a guard against tyrannical tendencies by our own national government.

But, says Weatherup, "The contemporary meaning of the Second Amendment is the same as it was at the time of its adoption. The federal government may regulate the National Guard, but may not disarm it against the will of state legislatures. Nothing in the Second Amendment, however, precludes Congress or the states from requiring licensing and registration; in fact there is nothing to stop an outright congressional ban on private ownership of all handguns and all rifles."

Weatherup, of course, is dead wrong, preposterously wrong. Indeed, as attorney and constitutional scholar Stephen P. Halbrook has noted, it is virtually impossible to find *any* support from the historical record of the time of the framing of the Constitution to support the thesis advanced by "collective" rights advocates. In his excellent study, *That Every Man Be Armed* (1984), Halbrook writes:

> In recent years it has been suggested that the Second Amendment protects the "collective" right of states to maintain militias, while it does not protect the right of "the people" to keep and bear arms. If anyone entertained this notion in the period during which the Constitution and Bill of Rights were debated and ratified, it remains one of the most closely guarded secrets of the eighteenth century, for no known writing surviving from the period between 1787 and 1791 states such a thesis.

America's Founding Fathers were not only extremely literate, well-read men, but prolific writers as well. Their private and public writings and records form a vast corpus from which we can derive an accurate understanding of the original intent behind any words that might be called into doubt today.[1] And, as Mr. Halbrook has indicated, any honest examination of the facts of history must acknowledge that on this important issue there was no debate; the framers of our Constitution were unanimous in the belief that private ownership of arms is an essential right of all free men.

Founders' words

While this diverse and immensely talented assemblage of intellects hotly debated numerous other points of political philosophy, economics, government, and law, on this question there is no evidence of the slightest controversy. Federalist and anti-Federalist alike stated their sentiments on the matter in unequivocal terms:

- Fisher Ames: "The rights of conscience, of bearing arms, of changing government, are declared to be inherent in the people."
- Zachariah Johnson: "[T]he people are not to be disarmed of their weapons. They are left in full possession of them. . . . The government will depend on the assistance of the people in the day of distress."
- Thomas Jefferson: "[N]o free man shall ever be debarred the use of arms."
- Richard Henry Lee: "To preserve liberty, it is essential that the whole body of the people always possess arms, and be taught alike, especially when young, how to use them."
- Patrick Henry: "Guard with jealous attention the public liberty. Suspect every one who approaches that jewel. Unfortunately, nothing will preserve it but downright force. Whenever you give up that force, you are ruined. . . . The great object is that every man be armed . . . everyone who is able may have a gun."

Tench Coxe, a prominent Federalist from Pennsylvania, was the equal of anti-Federalist Patrick Henry in defense of this right. In his influential essay, "An American Citizen," he declared:

> The powers of the sword are in the hands of the yeomanry of America from sixteen to sixty. The militia of these free commonwealths, entitled and accustomed to their arms, when compared with any possible army, must be tremendous and irresistible. Who are the militia? Are they not ourselves? . . . Congress have no power to disarm the militia. Their swords, and every other terrible implement of the soldier, are the birth-right of an American. . . . [T]he unlimited power of the sword is not in the hands of either the federal or state governments, but, where I trust in God it will ever remain, in the hands of the people.

Dr. Joyce Lee Malcolm, a professor of political history at Bentley College in Massachusetts, has contributed some of the most in-depth research on the English and American origins of the Second Amendment. In her timely book, *To Keep and Bear Arms: The Origins of an Anglo-American Right* (1994), she notes that Sir William Blackstone's four-volume *Commentaries on the Laws of England* was a big seller in the colonies, and that among the major American political writers between 1760 and 1805, "Blackstone was the most cited English writer." Writes Dr. Malcolm:

> Blackstone was firmly convinced that subjects needed to be armed to defend themselves and to avoid dependence on professional armies, but he also expanded the role of an armed citizenry beyond the individual's own preservation to the preservation of the entire constitutional structure. He dubbed the right of the people to be armed an "auxiliary" right of the subject that served "to protect and maintain inviolate the three great and primary rights, of personal security, personal liberty, and private property."

In February 1982, the Subcommittee on the Constitution of the U.S. Senate's Judiciary Committee published its examination into the controversies surrounding the Second Amendment in a report entitled *The Right to Keep and Bear Arms*. After extensive research into the annals of American legal and constitutional thought and due consideration to the arguments of all contemporary views, the subcommittee concluded: "The Second Amendment right to keep and bear arms therefore, is a right of the individual citizen to privately possess and carry in a peaceful manner firearms and similar arms. Such an 'individual rights' interpretation is in full accord with the history of the right to keep and bear arms, as previously discussed." Moreover, this interpretation, said the subcommittee report,

> accurately reflects the majority of the proposals which led up to the Bill of Rights itself. A number of state constitutions, adopted prior to or contemporaneously with the federal Constitution and Bill of Rights, similarly provided for a right of the people to keep and bear arms. If in fact this language creates a right protecting the states only, there might be a reason for it to be inserted in the federal Constitution but no reason for it to be inserted in state constitutions. State bills of rights necessarily protect only against action by the state, and by definition a state cannot infringe its own rights; to attempt to protect a right belonging to the state by inserting it in a limitation of the state's own powers would create an absurdity.

The Senate report also made note of the fact (as have many constitutional scholars) that those who are willing to so cavalierly dismiss the clear wording of "the right of the people" in the Second Amendment as meaning "the right of the state" to keep and bear arms, risk inviting the same interpretation for the identical wording elsewhere in the Bill of Rights. Will they concede that the same "right of the people" mentioned in the First and Fourth Amendments actually refers to the "right of the state" peaceably to assemble and the "right of the state" to be secure against unreasonable searches and seizures? To do so would be patently ludicrous, of course, but no more so than the same substitution for the Second Amendment.

Missing words

During the *Donahue* television show on the militia mentioned above, Phil Donahue had the text of the Second Amendment put up on the screen. However, it was Mr. Donahue's own rendition of the amendment, since the words "of the people" had been left out, without an ellipsis or any other indication that they were missing.

Wondering whether this represented gross ignorance, an enormous Freudian slip, or outright fraud on the part of Donahue and company, *The New American* decided to call the Sultan of Schlock himself for an explanation. *Donahue* supervising producer Albert Lewiton said Phil could not talk to us without clearance from media manager Rena Donlon. Ms. Donlon told *The New American* she would check on the matter and get back to us. Sure enough, a few minutes later she called to inform us that this was simply "a technician error" and that our call was the first time it had been brought to their attention.

Congress understood the term "militia" to include much more than the National Guard.

We suggested that their lame explanation was the kind of response that would have Mr. Donahue writhing in contortions of disbelief if given by a guest on his show. It was "only three words!" Ms. Donlon replied testily. "It was a simple error, and that's all there is to it." Yes, it was "only" three words, but three words critically important to a raging debate over a very crucial issue. And the omission of those specific words so conveniently buttressed Mr. Donahue's hostile view toward the Second Amendment, we noted, that "technician error" was a wholly inadequate excuse. Where were all of their high-paid editors, producers, and scriptwriters? Ms. Donlon was fuming. Would she be able to arrange for me to speak to Mr. Donahue himself? "Absolutely not!" she stated emphatically. As the Schlockmeister himself would say, "C'MON, Phil!"

So-called "civil libertarians," "scholars," and "jurists" have been attempting to wipe out the same words by redefining and interpreting them into oblivion. However, the historical record is so abundant and so remarkably clear that as long as a significant number of Americans can read and think for themselves, the intent of the Founders is obvious.

"The conclusion is thus inescapable," said the Senate subcommittee, "that the history, concept, and wording of the second amendment to the Constitution of the United States, as well as its interpretation by every major commentator and court in the first half-century after its ratification, indicates that what is protected is an individual right of a private citizen to own and carry firearms in a peaceful manner."

But what, then, is the relationship of this individual right to the militia, with which the individual right seems to be so closely bound? "The Second Amendment was meant to accomplish two distinct goals, each perceived as crucial to the maintenance of liberty," notes Dr. Joyce Malcolm. "First, it was meant to guarantee the individual's right to have arms for self-defense and self-preservation." Beyond this, she observes, "These privately owned arms were meant to serve a larger purpose as well." Dr. Malcolm writes:

> The second and related objective concerned the militia, and it is the coupling of these two objectives that has caused the most confusion. The customary American militia necessitated an armed

public and [James] Madison's original version of the amendment, as well as those suggested by the states, described the militia as either being "composed of" or "including" the body of the people. A select militia was regarded as little better than a standing army. The argument that today's National Guardsmen, members of a select militia, would constitute the *only* persons entitled to keep and bear arms has no historical foundation.

The whole people

Who are the militia? That was George Mason's exact question during debates at Virginia's own state constitutional convention. He answered his own rhetorical inquiry in these words: "They consist now of the whole people, except a few public officers." This was the common view of the Founders. Most of them had served in organized militias during the War for Independence and knew how essential these forces had been to the colonies' ultimate victory. They shared near unanimity also in the opinion that standing armies in times of peace posed a most serious threat to public liberty. Many of them also considered select militias as little less threatening than armies.

Noah Webster averred that a standing army could become oppressive only when it is "superior to any force that exists among the people," since otherwise it "would be annihilated on the first exercise of acts of oppression" by the armed people as a whole. Furthermore, said Webster:

> Before a standing army can rule, the people must be disarmed; as they are in almost every kingdom of Europe. The supreme power in America cannot enforce unjust laws by the sword; because the whole body of the people are armed and constitute a force superior to any band of regular troops that can be, on any pretense, raised in the United States.

Clearly, then, the Founding Fathers saw the militia as a protection not only against foreign invasion, but even more as a guard against tyrannical tendencies by our own national government.

Alexander Hamilton argued that a "small" army or select militia may be unavoidable. "If we mean to be a commercial people, or even to be secure on our Atlantic side, we must endeavor, as soon as possible, to have a navy," he wrote in #24 of *The Federalist Papers*, and added, "To this purpose there must be dockyards and arsenals; and for the defense of these, fortifications, and probably garrisons." If the power to raise armies in time of peace were not provided for in the Constitution, he asserted, "We must receive the blow before we could even prepare to return it." Still, if the army were a necessary evil, Hamilton concurred with his anti-Federalist opponents that the militia would provide a vital check against military usurpations. "If the federal government can command the aid of the militia in those emergencies which call for the military arm in support of the civil magistrate, it can better dispense with the employment of a different kind of force," Hamilton wrote in #29 of *The Federalist Papers*. For "If it cannot avail itself of the former, it will be obliged to recur to the latter. To render an army unnecessary will be a more certain method of preventing its existence than a thousand prohibitions on paper."

He continued:

This will not only lessen the call for military establishments, but if circumstances should at any time oblige the government to form an army of any magnitude that army can never be formidable to the liberties of the people while there is a large body of citizens, little if at all inferior to them in discipline and the use of arms, who stand ready to defend their own rights and those of their fellow-citizens. This appears to me the only substitute that can be devised for a standing army, and the best possible security against it, if it should exist.

You may have noticed something here: These men are talking about an armed citizenry, the militia, as a counterforce to the military and police powers of the government. How subversive!

Unless one has sound, moral public officials, the militiaman is potentially at the service of bad government.

James Madison was even more "extreme." Writing in *The Federalist Papers*, #46, he declared:

Extravagant as the supposition is, let it however, be made. Let a regular army, fully equal to the resources of the country, be formed; and let it be entirely at the devotion of the federal government: still it would not be going too far to say that the State governments with the people on their side would be able to repel the danger. The highest number to which, according to the best computation, a standing army can be carried in any country does not exceed one hundredth part of the whole number of souls; or one twenty-fifth part of the number able to bear arms. This proportion would not yield, in the United States, an army of more than twenty-five or thirty thousand men. To this would be opposed a militia amounting to near half a million of *citizens with arms in their hands, officered by men chosen from among themselves*, fighting for their common liberties and united and conducted by governments possessing their affections and confidence. It may well be doubted whether a militia thus circumstanced could ever be conquered by such a proportion of regular troops [emphasis added].

"Besides the advantage of being armed," Madison continued, "which the Americans possess over the people of almost every other nation, the existence of subordinate governments, to which the people are attached and by which the militia officers are appointed, forms a barrier against the enterprises of ambition, more insurmountable than any which a simple government of any form can admit of."

Article I, Section 8 of the U.S. Constitution, therefore, provides: "The Congress shall have power . . .":

To provide for calling forth the militia to execute the laws of the union, suppress insurrections and repel invasions:

To provide for organizing, arming, and disciplining, the militia, and for governing such part of them as may be employed in the service of the United States, reserving to the States respectively, the appointment of the officers, and the authority of training the militia according to the discipline prescribed by Congress [clauses 15 and 16].

Article II, Section 2 provides: "The President shall be commander-in-chief of the Army and Navy of the United States, and of the militia of the several States, when called into the actual service of the United States."

The Second Congress enacted the Militia Act of 1792, which required "every free able-bodied white male citizen of the respective states, resident therein, who is or shall be of the age of 18 years, and under the age of 45 years," to be enrolled in the militia and to be equipped with "a good musket," bayonet, and 24 rounds of ammunition. Did this mean that only those white males in the enrolled militia could keep and bear arms? Not at all, since all citizens were considered to be members of the general, unenrolled militia.

A national defense

Justice Joseph Story, in his highly esteemed *Commentaries on the Constitution* (1833) described the militia in this manner:

> The militia is the natural defense of a free country against foreign invasions, domestic insurrections, and domestic usurpations of power by rulers. It is against sound policy for a free people to keep up large military establishments and standing armies in time of peace, both from the enormous expenses, with which they are attended, and the facile means which they afford to ambitious and unprincipled rulers, to subvert the government, or trample the rights of the people. The right of a citizen to keep and bear arms has justly been considered the palladium of the liberties of the republic, since it offers a strong moral check against the usurpation and arbitrary power of rulers, and will generally, even if these are successful in the first instance, enable the people to resist and triumph over them.

What is all this talk about armed resistance to tyranny? Judge Story and Messrs. Madison, Hamilton, Lee, et al. are beginning to sound like some of these militia yahoos that Donahue, Dees, the ADL, and the *New York Times* are all in a dither over. But there is much more. Judge Thomas M. Cooley, another highly respected commentator on the Constitution, had this to say in his *General Principles of Constitutional Law* (1897):

> The right declared was meant to be a strong moral check against the usurpation and arbitrary power of rulers, and as a necessary and efficient means of regaining rights when temporarily overturned by usurpation.

> The Right is General—It may be supposed from the phraseology of this provision that the right to keep and bear arms was only guaranteed to the militia; but this would be an interpretation not warranted by the intent. . . . The meaning of the provision undoubtedly is that the people from whom the militia must be taken, shall have the right to keep and bear arms, and they need no permission or regulation of law for the purpose. . . .

The Militia Act of 1792 remained law for 111 years, into the 20th century. It was repealed in 1903 with passage of the "Dick Act," which created the National Guard—to substitute for a regular army, not for the militia. The new law retained the same definition of "all able-bodied males," but divided the militia into two classes, the "organized militia" and the "unorganized militia":

> (a) The militia of the United States consists of all able-bodied males at least 17 years of age and, except as provided in section 13 of title 32, under 45 years of age who are, or have made a declaration of intention to become, citizens of the United States. . . .
>
> (b) The classes of the militia are—
>
> > (1) the organized militia, which consists of the National Guard and the Naval Militia; and
> >
> > (2) the unorganized militia, which consists of members of the militia who are not members of the National Guard or the Naval Militia.

David Hardy, in *The Militia in the 20th Century* (1985) explained the significance of this development:

> It is clear from the debates over the Dick Act that the Congress understood the term "militia" to include much more than the National Guard. . . .
>
> The history of the 1903 Act thus makes it quite clear that Congress, in replacing the 1792 Act, did not intend to supplant the 1792 statute's definition of militia as virtually all able-bodied citizens. Nor did Congress believe that the National Guard it was creating was to be *the* militia, but only a *part* of the militia trained for instant response.

The wrong direction

However, the legislation was a major step on the road to full federalization of the militia, concentrating federal benefits (training, money grants, and surplus arms) upon the National Guard. This federalization was expanded with the National Defense Act of 1916, but failed to solve a major constitutional problem. Hardy explains:

> The Constitution authorizes Congress to provide "for calling forth the militia to execute the laws of the Union, suppress insurrections, and repel invasions." The three purposes were obviously chosen so as to keep the militia from being required to serve overseas—American laws can only be executed, insurrections against those laws suppressed, and invasions repelled, on American soil. The Attorney General of the United States had thus in 1912 ruled quite explicitly that the militia could not be compelled to serve outside the United States save in the most narrow of cases (hot pursuit of, or a "spoiling attack" upon, invaders). These three occasions, representing necessities of a strictly domestic character, plainly indicate that the services of the militia can be rendered only upon the soil of the United States or its territories.

When World War I came, President Woodrow Wilson could not "call" the Guard into foreign service under the militia clause, so he was given power to simply draft members of the organized militia into the regular army. In 1933 the National Guard Act technically fit the Guard into the Army clause. The House report on the 1933 Act clearly noted that its purpose was to amend "the National Defense Act so that the federally recognized National Guard shall at all times, whether in peace or in war, be a component of the Army of the United States. . . ." As noted in the *Congressional Record* of August 7, 1940, "Every National Guard man who takes the oath takes it with the understanding that he is part of the regular army and subject to the same obligations that may be imposed upon the regular army."

Thus the Subcommittee on the Constitution of the U.S. Senate Judiciary Committee reported in 1982:

> That the National Guard is not the "Militia" referred to in the second amendment is even clearer today. Congress has organized the National Guard under its power to "raise and support armies" and not its power to "Provide for organizing, arming and disciplining the Militia." This Congress chose to do in the interests of organizing reserve military units which were not limited in deployment by the strictures of our power over the constitutional militia, which can be called forth only "to execute the laws of the Union, suppress insurrections and repel invasions."

In *Perpich v. U.S. Department of Defense* (1990), the Supreme Court ruled that the states have very little recourse for opposing a presidential call up of their National Guard units, regardless of where in the world he may choose to send them, and no matter that there has been no presidential declaration of emergency. The Clinton Administration has announced plans to greatly increase the use of the National Guard in various "peacekeeping" missions around the globe. Clearly, by following the allure of federal funding, the states have converted virtually all of their state militias to organizations of the National Guard, which operate now at the behest of the White House. We have thus lost a very important constitutional check against the concentrated "power of the sword" that the framers warned would be so injurious to freedom.

The desire to recapture that power for the people and the states, as a safeguard against the encroachments and usurpations of an increasingly tyrannical federal government, is not a bad thing; indeed, as should be obvious from all of the foregoing, it is perfectly in line with the aims of our Founding Fathers. (George Washington and George Mason organized the Fairfax Independent Militia Company and many other Founders also were militia members.) Some two dozen states have retained some sort of residual state organized militia, though few of them, if any, are well-organized and well-regulated. These could be revitalized; new state militias could be organized in the remaining states. Even the Supreme Court, in its *Perpich* decision, agreed that the states could have their own militias, separate from the National Guard, and not subject to Guard call up— *if* these groups do not receive federal funds.

Serious considerations

However, even granting the historical and constitutional legitimacy of the militia, and the possible benefits of restoring that venerable institution to full vigor, some serious considerations remain that all patriots should ponder before embracing the militia movement as "the salvation of America," as some militia publications are wont to put it.

Under our U.S. Constitution, as already mentioned, Congress has power (Article I, Section 8) over organizing, arming, disciplining, and calling forth the militia; and, once they have been called forth into federal service, they are under the command of the President. When not in federal service, the militia traditionally has been under the authority of the governor and/or the state legislature, county, and city.

However, in order to receive federal funding under the National Defense Act of 1916, most states have passed legislation subsuming their organized state militias under the National Guard and have withdrawn authority for local governments to organize militias. While the new Congress may look considerably better than the old, it shouldn't be forgotten that the Republican leaders in the House and Senate have urged the President to step up U.S. involvement in the UN's war for the new world order in Bosnia. Would they support calling the militia into service in Bosnia, Rwanda, or elsewhere under Commander in Chief Bill Clinton? Might your governor or state legislature call out the militia to keep abortion clinics open so more babies can "safely" be killed? Are these far-out scenarios? Not when we consider what is already happening in this country.

There are genuinely sinister elements in the militia "movement" that cannot simply be brushed aside.

It quickly becomes apparent that unless one has sound, moral public officials, the militiaman is potentially at the service of bad government. The necessity then is for a plan of action to educate citizens so that they will elect and influence good leaders. Some militia leaders do stress civic responsibility and urge their members to vote, contact their elected officials, and become knowledgeable about important public issues. Others, though, proclaim that it is too late for these things and direct their followers instead to concentrate all of their time, money, and energy on stockpiling weapons, food, and survival gear, and on training for Armageddon. Neutralizing messages like this, of course, can become self-fulfilling prophecies. If patriots give up on restoring constitutional government and drop out of the daily fight for God, family, and country in order to spend all of their time oiling their guns and preparing for bloody conflict, they are helping to guarantee that tyranny will soon be upon us.

No reliable figures exist on the total number of individuals involved in militia groups nationwide. Bob Fletcher, a militia leader from Montana, claimed on the *Donahue* program that there are "ten million active members attending meetings" nationally. Most of the major media estimates have put the number at around 100,000. Even that estimate may be highly inflated and is impossible to verify. Norman Olson, commander of the Michigan Militia, claims a state membership of around 12,000 in 74 of the state's 83 counties. Olson said that the group's growth rate "has been phenomenal" and he expected to have brigades organized in the remainder of the counties by June 1995.

David Parker, commander of the Texas Constitutional Militia in the Orange-Beaumont-Port Arthur area, hazards an "unscientific" estimate of "quarter of a million to half a million" active militia members in Texas. He claims "about 80" members in his local unit and says that over 200 interested citizens attended his public presentation in Beaumont in December 1994.

We are indeed living in perilous times, times that demand of all patriots not only courage and steadfast determination, but also wisdom and perseverance.

One Florida organizer who requested anonymity said that there are "at a minimum, 35,000" actively involved in the Sunshine State and "ten times" that number who are supporters. Another Florida leader who also asked not to be named claims that there are 100,000 to 250,000 organized statewide in militias, and "many times" that number not formally attached. We found similarly varying figures in most other states.

Militia organizations come in all shapes, sizes, and flavors. Some are strictly local affairs with no affiliation to state or national organizations; others are affiliated in a formal state or regional structure. Some are secret "underground" groups; others are very public and high profile, appearing regularly on radio and television and in the print media. Some make a point of going to local and state public officials and law enforcement personnel to educate and work with them on matters of concern to the militia; others view all authorities with hostility. Some regularly assemble for drills and exercises with arms on public or private lands; others forbid those activities as illegal and inappropriate for their members.

Some militia groups recognize no public authority whatsoever over their organizations and advocate confrontational tactics such as marching en masse, armed and in "uniform," on city halls, police stations, FBI offices, schools, and other government agencies. In 1994, Linda Thompson, an Indianapolis attorney who had appointed herself "Acting Adjutant General, Unorganized Militia of the United States of America," urged militia groups nationwide to converge on Washington, DC on September 19th (with their guns) to charge members of Congress with treason and enforce her "Ultimatum," a list of her "commands" to repeal certain laws. If her insurrection had materialized, with thousands of armed "militiamen" swarming Capitol Hill, President Clinton and the Establishment press would have been handed, on a silver platter, "proof" of the need for more drastic gun control laws and emergency police powers.

Thompson was arrested in July 1994 in Indianapolis for blocking a street with her vehicle in an attempt to stop Hillary Clinton's traveling health care caravan. According to news reports, police seized two pistols from her person and found a rifle with hundreds of rounds of ammunition in her car.

The ADL report, *Armed and Dangerous*, claims that Thompson is "an influential figure in the militia movement nationally," and that even though support for her planned Washington, DC insurrection failed to materialize, "her standing in the militia movement apparently remains undiminished." Our investigations, to the contrary, indicate that Linda Thompson is almost thoroughly discredited among most militia groups.

However, she still operates a computer bulletin board which dispatches rumors that find their way into many militia circles. In our special investigative report, "Fact and Fiction," in the October 31, 1994, issue of *The New American*, we reported on the many wild and unsubstantiated rumors concerned with invading UN troops, "black helicopters," and other alarming stories that have been causing near panic in many parts of the country. The more sensational-minded militia groups use these stories to whip up excitement and assist in recruitment.

As we mentioned at the beginning of this viewpoint, there are genuinely sinister elements in the militia "movement" that cannot simply be brushed aside as inventions of the controlled media and the radical-left lobbyists. Besides those like Linda Thompson who attempt to translate widespread anti-Washington feelings, outrage over Waco [site of the burning of Branch Davidian leader David Koresh's compound], and anger over the Brady bill [1994 gun-control legislation] into dangerous insurrectionist schemes, there are also veteran racist and fascist figures who are trying to use and promote the growing militia movement. Tom Stetson, Louis Beam, Pete Peters, Adam Troy Mercer, and other longtime leaders in groups such as the Aryan Nations, the Order, the KKK, Identity, and other virulently racist and violent organizations are making the rounds at militia gatherings, trying to recruit new followers and sow their gospels of hate. These and other dangerous demagogues are adept at grabbing the spotlight and encouraging violent confrontations and provocations. Militia leaders in several states have said that they are very concerned about the efforts of these individuals and organizations to disrupt, infiltrate, and/or take over militia units, or to taint the militia by association.

"Underground" incitement

Scrapes with the law have already occurred. In July 1994, federal Bureau of Alcohol, Tobacco, and Firearms (ATF) agents arrested four members of the Blue Ridge Hunt Club in Virginia for possession of illegal firearms and silencers. News reports referred to the group as a militia. ATF officials claim the men were planning terrorist actions and a raid on the National Guard armory in Pulaski.

In August 1994, a police officer in Fowlerville, Michigan made a 2:30 a.m. traffic stop of a driver whose car had strayed over the center line. Inside were three young men in camouflage uniforms, with their faces painted in camouflage paint and a loaded 9mm pistol clip lying on the seat. They were arrested and found to be in possession of the following loaded weapons: 9mm, AK-47, M-1, M-14, and .357. Fowlerville Police Chief Gary Krause said that they were also in possession of "over 700 rounds of ammunition, including tracer and armor-piercing types, gas masks, night-vision goggles, other military equipment, and handwritten notes on surveilling police stations." Krause said the notes also discussed dealing with opponents "with extreme prejudice," a term understood in military circles to mean assassination.

The men were charged with violations of state laws and released on bail. When they did not show up for their arraignment, warrants were issued for their arrests. Some 30 to 40 individuals claiming to be militia members did show up at the arraignment, however, to protest the arrest.

Chief Krause says they taunted and insulted his officers, calling them "punks with badges" and threatening to "shoot the cop next time they're stopped." This, understandably, has not made Chief Krause a big fan of the militia.

Michigan Militia Commander Norman Olson says the men arrested and the protesters were not his men. "They were part of an 'underground' group," Olson said. "We don't operate that way. We are a 'well regulated' militia and will not let our people break the laws. Members are under strict orders not to carry weapons; we use the same procedures and regulations as the military."

According to Olson, his organization supports local law enforcement. "We are for restoration and liberation, not revolution. We are for the Constitution, jury trials, county government, state sovereignty, and for reestablishing the county sheriff as the highest law enforcement authority in the state." Everything they do, says Olson, is "completely legal" and in accordance with state law and the Constitution.

Other militia experts are not so sure. M. Samuel Sherwood, founder and director of the United States Militia Association (USMA) in Blackfoot, Idaho, believes that many (if not most) militia groups are "on very shaky legal ground." Most states have laws, he says, that prohibit private paramilitary groups, and "simply calling yourself a militia doesn't make you one" and thereby exempt you from those laws. "They may think what they are doing is legal and constitutional, but they will probably find out differently," he says. Sherwood is the author of *The Guarantee of the 2nd Amendment*, which has served as a handbook and organizing manual for much of the growing movement. He has helped set up USMA affiliates in 12 counties in Idaho and in ten other states. He has interested parties forming affiliates in 35 other states. As such, it might seem odd that he would be alarmed at the success of a movement he has played such a large role in launching. But Sherwood believes that many of those using his material misunderstand some very important points of principle and law.

Working within the law

Sherwood points out that under the U.S. Constitution and federal and state laws, all able-bodied citizens are already members of the "unorganized militia." However, when private citizens begin organizing into armed groups without state sanction, "they are just private armies which are in violation of the law" in most states. In Idaho, for instance, he points out, the law (Idaho 46-802) provides that "no body of men" other than the National Guard and the "organized militia" called into service by the state may assemble with arms. Texas law (Chapter 431.010a) provides:

> Except as provided by Subsection (b), a body of persons other than
> the regularly organized state military forces or the troops of the
> United States may not associate as a military company or organiza-
> tion or parade in public with firearms in a municipality of the state.

According to Sherwood, similar laws are on the books in many states and, sooner or later, are bound to be used against those groups calling themselves militias. Many individuals involved with these organizations also don't understand, he says, that their careless use of words like "armed resistance" and their public utterances about willfully flouting the laws may fall under the definition of sedition and may end up being used against them in federal court.

Unlike militia groups that are often seen on television news programs, Sherwood's USMA units do not drill or carry weapons. "That would be totally inappropriate," he says. "We believe in county, city, and state militia units that have the charter, sanction, or approval of the sheriffs, county commissioners, or whoever the local political authority is, based upon law." That means, he says, educating citizens and working to change state law so that militias can be formed again *legally*, under the proper governing authority—*not* under the control of private groups like the USMA.

"It is better to suffer under unjust laws than to resort to anarchy and lawlessness," cautions Sherwood. "The suffering is an indication that something is wrong and should motivate people to change what is wrong. If you simply evade the bad law, you allow the injustices to multiply and the 'rule of law' to be mocked."

Sherwood's approach has won him brickbats (and even a death threat) from some of the more radical militia proponents, but it has earned him respect from many others—including public officials. Idaho's Secretary of State Pete Cenarrusa has met with Sherwood and has "read an article of his [on the militia] that seems to make sense." "I'm willing to listen to their proposals," Mr. Cenarrusa said, "but anything done will have to be done in accordance with state law. As long as they do that— are in accord with state law, the state constitution, the U.S. Constitution—I think it's a good thing."

While the legal standing of many of the militia organizations may be uncertain, there should be no uncertainty about this: Bill Clinton, [U.S. attorney general] Janet Reno, [FBI director] Louis Freeh, and their federal minions can be counted on to fully exploit any and all incidents involving militias, and to be monitoring the actions and rhetoric of militia members. Together with the media, they will attempt to construct the spectre of a terrible armed threat amongst us. Unfortunately, there appear to be many in the ranks of the militia movement who will play right into their hands. And if that doesn't happen on its own, the militias provide the perfect medium for federal *agents provocateurs* to instigate outrageous offenses that can be used to justify even more draconian gun control laws and police-state repression.

We are indeed living in perilous times, times that demand of all patriots not only courage and steadfast determination, but also wisdom and perseverance. Those who are intent on transforming the United States into a socialist cog in a totalitarian new world order want, above all, to engender a spirit of despair, hopelessness, hatred, conflict, and anarchy. They want the law-abiding to give up on the constitutional system and to take rash courses of action and reaction that will label them as "rebels" and "enemies" of law and order. Those who fall into this trap are tragic fools. The right to keep and bear arms must be defended, yes. But free men can best preserve that right and every other by exercising the rights which they still have to speak, to write, to pray, to assemble, to vote, and to educate. We *must* stay the course and resist all temptations to despair or reckless folly.

Notes

1. Following are but a few of the numerous documentary sources pertaining to the origins of the Second Amendment which are available at many large libraries: *The Documentary History of the Ratification of the Constitution*, by Merrill Jensen (1976); *Documents Illustrative of the Formation of the Union of the American States* (U.S. House of Representatives Document 398; 1927, U.S. Government Printing Office); *Debates in the Several State Conventions on the Adoption of the Federal Constitution*, edited by Jonathan Elliot, five volumes (1863); *Birth of the Federal Constitution: A History of the New Hampshire Convention*, by Joseph Walker (1888); *Debates and Other Proceedings of the Convention of Virginia*, by David Robertson (1805); *The Making of the American Republic: The Great Documents, 1774–1789*, edited by Charles Callan Tansill (1927); *The Records of the Federal Convention of 1787*, edited by Max Farrand, three volumes (1911); *The Bill of Rights: A Documentary History*, by B. Schwartz (1971); *American Political Writings During the Founding Era 1760–1805*, by Charles S. Hyneman and Donald S. Lutz (1983); *A People Numerous and Armed*, by John Shy (1976).

5

The Militia Movement Is Dangerous

Scott McLemee

Scott McLemee is a contributing editor for In These Times, *a biweekly liberal publication. McLemee has written about right-wing movements and organizations for the* New York Times, Covert Action Quarterly, *and* Against the Current.

The new militia movement embraces a variety of potentially dangerous beliefs, including white supremacy, antigovernment conservatism, and opposition to abortion and gun control. Militias have been linked to violent antiabortion groups and the 1995 bombing of an Oklahoma City federal building. Despite its paramilitary orientation, the militia movement continues to garner recognition and win support, including that of elected officials.

With more than 40 women's clinics bombed since 1977, right-wing terrorism ought to be a widely acknowledged fact of American political life by now. In fact, information on manufacturing fertilizer bombs—like the one used on April 19, 1995, at the Alfred P. Murrah Federal Building in Oklahoma City—can be found in a manual distributed by Army of God, a highly secretive anti-abortion group that bombed clinics during the mid-'80s. Yet the national psyche has seemed unwilling to confront the reality of domestic terrorism.

The explosion that destroyed the federal building, however, was almost certainly the work of a paramilitary cell from the self-described "unorganized militia" movement—a right-wing current that has rallied around April 19 as a symbol of government tyranny and citizen resistance.

In the aftermath of the bombing, the media has scrambled to provide information and analysis on the militias. Yet those who study the right wing have been aware of the movement's growth since 1994; and in talking with activists and researchers who have been monitoring the militias, one soon detects a note of frustration in their voices. After all, they spent months warning about the emergence of paramilitary units in dozens of states across the country. And as observers from Georgia to Montana

Scott McLemee, "Public Enemy," *In These Times*, May 15, 1995. Reprinted by permission.

noted, individuals with deep connections to the racist right have played a significant role in the growth of the movement.

Those who have closely observed militia activity suspected it was only a matter of time before some act of political violence occurred. But no one quite expected an incident of the magnitude of Oklahoma City. Given the enormity of that event, it was not surprising that the media, after largely ignoring the militia movement, would tend to label its adherents "extremists." Yet many people who study the right find it unwise to treat the militias as the "lunatic fringe" of an otherwise "respectable" conservative movement. Its issues, strategies and rhetoric overlap with those of "mainstream" right groups. And the movement will still be around after the cameras and reporters have gone.

A movement, not an organization

Perhaps the most difficult thing to convey about the militia is the paradoxical *newness* of this movement. Paradoxical, because the militia has deep roots in traditions of right-wing paramilitarism—and many of its preoccupations are rooted in classical themes of conservative anger at big government, sifted through the paranoiac filter of conspiracy theory. Yet these old themes have been put together in an innovative and powerful way. The militias have taken shape as a *movement*, not an organization—and various currents within the militias fuse and overlap in different combinations.

Militia ideology links up age-old visions of worldwide conspiracy and race war with the newer ideologies of the anti-abortion and anti-environmentalist movements. And unusual interpretations of the Bible and the Constitution have found new audiences among the tens of thousands of people in and around the militias. It seems, at times, a doctrinal free-for-all. And that makes generalizing about militia ideology a somewhat hazardous business.

The militias first began springing up in early 1994, rallying to fight the outrages of the Brady Bill—the first federal gun-control legislation to become law. They took as their charter the Second Amendment to the Constitution: "A well-regulated militia being necessary to the security of a free state, the right of the people to keep and bear arms shall not be infringed." The militias advocate what Dennis Henigan of the Center to Prevent Handgun Violence has termed "the insurrectionist theory of the Second Amendment." In its literature, the Militia of Montana insists that the "right to bare (sic) arms" requires preparation "to use them in military confrontation. Not just pack them around the house, yard or forest."

But this preoccupation with the Second Amendment is only part of a much more comprehensive legal theory called "Constitutionalism," which often resembles the "states rights" arguments of the old white supremacist movement. "Constitutionalists" distinguish carefully between "White Common Law Citizens of the State" and those inferior Americans whose citizenship was conferred by the 14th Amendment (the one extending constitutional protection to newly freed slaves).

Constitutionalism does far more than merely reinforce racist views within the militia movement: It underwrites an individualist philosophy espousing the virulent hatred of government. Constitutionalists are prone to filing impressive-sounding (but legally meaningless) documents renouncing their citizenship from "the foreign jurisdiction known as the municipal corporation of the District of Columbia." They then refuse to register their automobiles, use a Social Security number, or pay taxes. The highest power they recognize is the state—or, in some cases, the county—government. This posture makes a confrontation between heavily armed Constitutionalists and "unconstitutional" civil authority more or less inevitable.

The movement's theology is every bit as innovative as its legal theory. Its religious outlook is emerging as an important link between the militias and the violence-prone wing of the anti-abortion movement, which in turn moves them closer to the pale of the mainstream right. Adherents of Christian Identity—a white-supremacist theology that regards Jews as "the seed of Satan" and non-whites as "pre-Adamic mud people" without souls—have proselytized within some militias. According to Tom Burghardt of the Bay Area Coalition for Our Human Rights, Identity followers are a growing presence within the anti-abortion movement.

Likewise, the Christian Reconstructionism movement—which advocates religious dictatorship, with the death penalty for homosexuals, among others—is another theological current within the campaign against reproductive choice. Randall Terry, founder of Operation Rescue, has recently been working with the Reconstructionist-linked U.S. Taxpayers Party, which supports both the killing of abortion doctors and the growth of local militias.

Fred Clarkson, of Planned Parenthood's Public Policy Institute in New York City, argues that the anti-choice movement has been critical in the formation of various militias. "All are anti-abortion, period," he explains. "There is some networking between the militias and the anti-abortion movement, though it isn't clear how much. People come to it with different ideologies, but it would be a mistake to see this as a *secular* right-wing movement. It's religious, varying from white-supremacist theology to ordinary Baptist fundamentalism."

The militias have taken shape as a movement, *not an organization—and various currents within the militias fuse and overlap.*

There is a religious dimension, too, in the militia's fear of the United Nations. Pat Robertson's best-selling book *New World Order* explained to millions of readers the role of the U.N. as a tool of the various secret societies now controlling the world. The United Nations, never popular in conservative circles, has taken the place formerly occupied by World Communism in the demonology of the right.

As political issues, gun control and the United Nations might not seem to have much in common. But to militia members the link is obvious: both represent attacks on freedom, violating the sovereignty of the individual and the nation, respectively.

For the Militia of Montana, at least, the Brady Bill is an integral part of the worldwide conspiracy. The group's literature quotes Sarah Brady—

whose husband, Press Secretary James Brady, took an assassin's bullet meant for Ronald Reagan—as saying, "Our task of creating a *socialist* America can only succeed when those who would resist us have been *totally disarmed.*" It is the sort of spurious quote that once circulated in anti-Communist tracts; there, it was attributed to Vladimir Lenin, or John F. Kennedy, or [U.S. Communist Party leader] Gus Hall. But now, without the threat of "the international communist conspiracy" as an ideological glue, right-wing ideologues have had to improvise.

Growth in 1994

Substantial militia organizations began appearing in Michigan and Montana in the spring of 1994. By the summer, militia organizers were attracting hundreds of participants to meetings. The gatherings typically included lectures and videotapes concerning the Federal siege that ended in the fiery deaths of 78 Branch Davidians at their compound in Waco, Texas, on April 19, 1993. According to Beth Hawkins (who did some of the earliest reporting on the movement for Detroit's *Metro Times* weekly newspaper), by fall 1994 the Michigan Militia "credibly could claim 10,000 members, the vast majority of them drawn to the group because its leaders described it as a forum to protect the Second Amendment."

It has proved difficult to estimate the size of the movement nationally. There have been reports of militia organizations in every state except Hawaii—though in some cases, the "organization" may consist of little more than an irate citizen with a post-office box. Observers estimate that militia members nationwide number in the tens of thousands, though such figures overlook the much larger base of those who support the militias, even if they do not join.

To judge from its literature, videotapes and public meetings, the overwhelming majority of members are white working-class or lower-middle-class men. There is no central organization, though several federations or networks link them. Indeed, part of what makes the militias attractive to recruits is their highly decentralized form of organization—the very opposite of the federal tyranny they are designed to fight. Local militias are connected up nationally by computer bulletin boards and fax networks and at least some encouragement for the militias comes from talk radio.

In Colorado Springs, Colorado, talk-show host Chuck Baker found in the militias his way to outrush Rush Limbaugh, as Leslie Jorgenson reported in an issue of *EXTRA!* In 1994, Baker added a new sound effect to his radio program: the "kching, kching" of a firing pin. "Suddenly, Baker began discussing the need for an armed revolution to take out the 'slime balls' in Congress and bureaucrats 'who are too stupid to get a job.'"

Additional support for the militias came from the "Radio Free America" show, hosted by Tom Valentine, a supporter of the Liberty Lobby, an anti-Semitic "populist" group based in Washington, D.C.

By early fall of 1994, the Liberty Lobby's widely circulated tabloid the *Spotlight* ran regular articles claiming that United Nations troops were being deployed throughout the Midwest and Southwestern United States. In Arizona, the lead headline on September 12 read, "Armed Patriots Confront UN Unit"—one of several reports on alleged encounters between militias and foreign troops. At an October rally in Lansing, Michigan, hundreds of militia members gathered to protest the raising of a U.N. flag at a city hall.

Throughout the militia movement, accounts of mysterious "black copters"—also part of the reported U.N. maneuvers—began to circulate. "They have been chasing people, hovering over houses, following cars on the roads, killing birds and cattle, and pointing what appeared to be guns at people," as the *Spotlight* explained.

As such reports multiplied, some sectors of the movement wanted to quit drilling and begin to fight. In September 1994, near Lansing, police stopped a car that had been weaving across the road; inside, they found three militia members wearing blackface and camouflage, carrying night goggles, semiautomatic weapons and 700 rounds of ammunition. That same month, Linda Thompson—an Indiana attorney and self-proclaimed Adjutant General of the Unorganized Militia of the United States—called for armed "patriots" to descend on Washington, D.C., and mete out rough justice to the "traitors" in Congress.

Thompson calculated that, out of 2 million U.S. troops, half were abroad, and half of those remaining weren't trained for combat. "The best [the government] could come up with, of all the troops they could muster, would be 500,000 people," she explained on Chuck Baker's radio show. "They would be outnumbered five to one, if only one percent of the country went up against them."

This was the first call for national action by the militias. Since Thompson is a prominent figure within the movement, her call to arms was widely discussed among militia members.

The overwhelming majority of members are white working-class or lower-middle-class men.

Thompson also set the important precedent of using Waco as a rallying cry in the war on government. The videos circulated by her American Justice Federation portrayed the siege at Waco as an early battle between oppressed citizens and federal tyranny; these tapes were a staple of militia recruitment around the country. But Thompson's insurrectionary arithmetic failed to persuade many people that the time had come. Plans for the September mobilization quickly fell apart.

The proposed march on Washington by armed militia supporters raised misgivings within the far right—even among those who agreed entirely that a worldwide conspiracy was ready to make America into a totalitarian state. Yet the movement continues to circulate manuals that laud the use of force to protect individual freedoms threatened by government.

"A public-relations announcement may or may not be necessary after an assassination or a failed attempt," the *U.S. Militiaman's Handbook* by Dan Shoemaker helpfully advises. The same book provides the words to be read on another special occasion the militiaman will, presumably, face sooner or later: "You (call the prisoner by name, if you know his name) have committed treason against the United States Constitution and against your fellow citizens and members of the United States Militia. You are now executed."

Despite the movement's paramilitary orientation, it is making steady inroads into a broader political base and even finding allies among some elected officials. A recent development among militia supporters, according to Noah Chandler of the Center for Democratic Renewal in Atlanta, is the series of "patriot conventions" held by various local militias around the country. He sent me the program for the Restore Our Liberty Convention held in Atlanta in mid-March 1995. Among the featured speakers were state senators from Colorado and California, members of both houses of the Georgia legislature, a Nevada county commissioner, and a retired member of the Washington state supreme court.

Recent "patriot conventions" show that the movement, though purposely decentralized, may be inching toward some kind of political expression. As Chandler stressed, "Local militias don't affiliate the way other groups might, to form a national organization. But you do have people traveling across the country to attend these events. That way they can keep the aura of the 'unorganized militia,' yet be connected up."

In Montana

Before April 19, 1995, it was easy enough to ignore people who believed that U.N. troops would shortly be imposing martial law on the United States. Such a movement, no matter what strange plans it makes, is distant enough from ordinary life to be no part of reality as we know it. Not so for Ken Toole, a progressive organizer I spoke with by phone in late April 1995. He works out of the office of the Montana Human Rights Network (MHRN), which is located in the city of Helena on a street called Last Chance Gulch.

Around 2,000 members of MHRN conduct educational programs against racism and intolerance throughout the state. The network also publishes a newsletter reporting on developments in Montana and nearby Idaho (home of several far-right groups). At the start of its work in 1990, the network quickly drew the ire of the Christian Right. But things got worse in early 1994 when the Militia of Montana (which sports the heartwarming acronym MOM) came on the scene.

Initially, Toole says, meetings held around issues such as the Brady Bill and the Waco siege drew large audiences throughout the state. One gathering at Kalispell in early March 1994 attracted 800 people; at least five other meetings in cities and towns throughout Montana during the first half of 1994 had 200 or more participants. As the Network reports in *A Season of Discontent: Militias, Constitutionalists and the Far Right in Montana,* "After being exposed to the more extreme positions of the organizers, the number of people who come to a second or third meeting tends to drop off."

Even so, by late spring 1994 a hard core had formed around the Trocchmann brothers, John and David, who had previously been active in Aryan Nations—an anti-Semitic and white supremacist religious group that has in recent years devoted considerable energy to missionary work among skinheads.

The Trocchmanns say there are 10,000 members in MOM—a figure state militia leaders seem fond of claiming. I asked Toole for the Network estimate. After some hesitation, he guessed that there could be as many as 500 militia members in the state, not counting sympathizers who don't actually belong. Montana has more than its share of far-rightists, including Klan members, tax resisters and "Constitutionalists" who hold court to try and sentence government officials they find traitorous.

The size of the organization may be an open question, but MOM is without a doubt one of the main sources of literature for the militia movement nationally. MOM advertises its material in the *Spotlight*, including a videotape suggesting that the government is training the Crips and the Bloods to confiscate the weapons of (white) Americans. MOM says it can fax information to half a million militia followers in 30 minutes through its Patriot Fax Network. Indeed, the editor of one militia newspaper, *Veritas*, complains of arriving at the office to find pages of unsubstantiated rumors pouring off the fax machine, with "the large black letters MOM staring up at me" from the pile.

As Toole describes it, the militia has made intimidation of the MHRN a small but regular part of its work. He tells of how, during the spring of 1994, a public school administrator and some teachers in a small town invited the network to give a couple of background presentations on the religious right. Throughout the day, he found picket lines of 30 or 40 people—including militia members who, along with supporters of the White Aryan Resistance, showed up at meetings to videotape participants and filibuster. This has become a fact of network life: fairly low-key but persistent harassment of both activists and those who attend the meetings.

Toole sounds a lot more cheerful than someone in his position has any reason to be. He suggests that it would be good for me to talk to someone involved in local network activity, and directs me to Carlotta Grandstaff, who lives and works in Hamilton, a small city of around 20,000 people.

Like Americans across the country, Grandstaff had been following events in Oklahoma and the national coverage of the militias. Throughout our phone interview she spoke, much as Toole had, of the militias' steady war of nerves—but only when discussing the media did she seem actually to get annoyed. The mainstream media's message in the wake of the bombing appeared to be that people outside the Eastern cities were all right-wingers or gun nuts. "The militias," she said, "have been very intimidating to ordinary people out here."

The movement . . . is making steady inroads into a broader political base and even finding allies among some elected officials.

And even after the bombing, the images of the militias on television seemed to trivialize the movement. "It's not a bunch of guys running around in the woods with guns, playing GI Joe on the weekend," she insisted. "It goes a lot deeper than that. They really think that they are saving the world from the evil federal government."

The Hamilton chapter of the network formed in response to Aryan Nations activity in the area. When MOM began recruiting around the state in 1994, Grandstaff says, many Hamilton residents looked to the network for some kind of response. The group gathered 900 signatures on a petition, published in the local newspaper, denouncing the threat of violence the militia posed. Then, in March 1995, the network organized a Community Unity Day to promote tolerance and democratic values. Even though it was very quickly put together, it drew 200 people—including some militia members who heckled. Few of the monthly meetings are held in public anymore; otherwise, right-wingers "just show up and filibuster."

A militia member, Al Hamilton, charged in 1994 with felony intimidation of a district judge, was due to be released on bail in 1995. Grandstaff mentions the fear that, once released, Hamilton and his associates in the North American Militia may provoke some confrontation with the police or the state. A letter written by the Indiana-based North American Militia had denounced the judge as a "corrupt official" who "might take notice when you see officers return in body bags."

Leaderless resistance and the future of militias

Everyone now wonders about the future of the movement. But experienced militia-watchers are quite reluctant to speculate about the direction it might take next. The phenomenon is simply too diverse and complex, and the situation after Oklahoma too volatile. "What's interesting to me about this development, the militia movement, is that it *is* developing," Fred Clarkson of Planned Parenthood said. "It's a dynamic process, not a static thing. It's less than two years old, and it's changing all the time. Anti-abortion, white supremacy, paramilitary—these separate categories aren't really so separate here. And that makes it hard to figure out."

But for at least some in the militia movement, the developments in Oklahoma seem almost a godsend. The program of "leaderless resistance" advocated by Louis Beam—a former Texas Klan leader and Aryan Nations theorist—bears striking similarities to what appears to have been the approach of the group responsible for the bombing. And the federal crackdown may purge the movement of those Beam considers amateurs.

Beam's document on leaderless resistance, first published in 1992, reads very much like a blueprint for the militia movement itself:

> All members of phantom cells or individuals will tend to react to objective events in the same way through usual tactics of resistance. Organs of information distribution such as newspapers, leaflets, computers, etc., which are widely available to all, keep each person informed of events, allowing for a planned response that will take many variations. No one need issue an order to anyone. Those idealists truly committed to the cause of freedom will act when they feel the time is ripe, or will take their cue from others who precede them.

But the program for "leaderless resistance" also sounds, at times, like a criticism of the militias. It counsels "avoidance of *all* contact with the front men for the federals—the news media." It demands that "patriots" break down into very small units of around a half-dozen guerrillas: "[T]he *last* thing federal snoops want, if they had any choice in the matter, is a thousand different small phantom cells opposing them."

Beam considers existing right-wing groups necessary but not capable of adequately challenging the government and other forces of tyranny against "our race, culture, and heritage." Small terror squads—Beam's "phantom cells"— would be much more effective. "Those who join organizations to play 'let's pretend' or who are 'groupies,'" he writes, "will quickly be weeded out."

These ideas may well become more common within the militia movement after Oklahoma, as justifiable fears about infiltration join the more familiar paranoia about the New World Order.

Within 24 hours of the bombing, several militia leaders around the country claimed that the files on the Waco incident had been stored at the federal building in Oklahoma City. The statements appeared almost simultaneously: a tribute, perhaps, to the effectiveness of the fax networks.

[The Militia of Montana] says it can fax information to half a million militia followers in 30 minutes through its Patriot Fax Network.

And also a sign of how neatly events can be fitted into the conspiratorial scenario. As strange as the ideas of the movement seem to anyone not living in the universe of the militias, this much seems clear: It is a movement prone to violence, but remarkably resilient—and nothing if not imaginative. Shortly after the bombing, it had absorbed the event into its own ideology, once again finding evidence of federal tyranny. As the Militia of Montana representative I spoke with explained, the Bureau of Alcohol, Tobacco and Firearms sacrificed four of its own agents at Waco; why wouldn't they sacrifice a couple of hundred citizens in Oklahoma? He took my silence after this interpretation as skepticism. But in fact, I was just speechless.

6

Citizen Militias Can Become Violent

Chip Berlet and Matthew N. Lyons

Chip Berlet is an analyst at Political Research Associates in Cambridge, Massachusetts. Matthew N. Lyons is a freelance writer and independent historian. They are the authors of Too Close for Comfort: Rightwing Populism, Scapegoating, and Fascist Potentials in U.S. Politics.

Armed militias are the militant branch of the five-million-member right-wing Patriot movement. Individuals within this movement adhere to a variety of ideologies, including white supremacy and Christian fundamentalism. Although it was the most devastating, the 1995 bombing of an Oklahoma City federal building was not the first violent act linked to militias and it may not be the last. Some of the militia members' grievances, such as economic hardship and government intrusiveness, are legitimate. Unless society addresses these grievances, scapegoating by militias against their enemies will increase and may lead to violence and murder.

We have been studying the armed militias with a group of more than 100 analysts and reporters for many months. The issue for us was never if there was going to be violence, but how much violence would be tolerated by society before there was a decision to do something about it. The violence has been against health clinics and reproductive-rights activists, environmental activists, people of color, gays and lesbians, and Jews. Threats against government officials have become commonplace, especially in the Pacific Northwest.

Many of us thought that April 19, 1995, would bring a physical confrontation of some sort, given that Waco is the central icon of this movement. [On April 19, 1993, David Koresh and scores of his Branch Davidian religious sect followers died when their compound near Waco, Texas, burned during a federal raid.] No one imagined a horror of the magnitude of what happened in Oklahoma City.

The bombing of the Alfred P. Murrah federal building on April 19 and the reported involvement of perpetrators linked to armed rightwing mili-

Chip Berlet and Matthew N. Lyons, "Militia Nation," *Progressive*, June 1995. Reprinted with permission of the *Progressive*, 409 E. Main St., Madison, WI 53703.

tias finally made the danger of these groups evident to all. But the warning signs were there all along.

The growth of armed militias has been rapid, with new units appearing on a weekly basis. An educated guess about the number of militia members ranges from 10,000 to 40,000. There is at least one militia unit up and running in forty states, with militia organizing most likely happening in all fifty states.

Anyone with an ear to the ground could have heard the rumblings.

The Oklahoma bombing was not by any means the first act of public violence with connections to the armed militias and the Patriot movement they grow out of. John Salvi, who is accused of shooting reproductive-rights workers in Brookline, Massachusetts, in 1994, told his former employer that he was interested in the armed militias. And Francisco Duran, who was convicted of spraying the White House with bullets, was linked to the Patriot movement and armed militias.

In 1993, even before the militias had settled on a name, alternative journalists began writing about them. Small research groups issued report after report, but no one seemed to be listening. The best early research came from such groups as the Coalition for Human Dignity, People Against Racist Terror, Western States Center, Institute for First Amendment Studies, Alternet, the Montana Human Rights Network, Political Research Associates, the Center for Democratic Renewal, and many others.

The first national groups that tried to get reporters to pay attention to the threat included Planned Parenthood, Greenpeace, the Sierra Club, and the Environmental Working Group. The first national conference on the threat posed by the militias was held near Seattle in January 1995 and was organized by the Northwest Coalition Against Malicious Harassment.

The Southern Poverty Law Center wrote to Janet Reno on October 25, 1994, alerting her to the danger of the militias. The Anti-Defamation League of B'nai B'rith and the American Jewish Committee published reports on the militias.

So how were the warnings of scores of groups and hundreds of people so systematically ignored by government officials? Activists and researchers had been pleading with Congress to hold hearings on the ongoing rightwing violence for years. It took a stack of bodies to force the hearing onto the calendar, and now we see that Congressional attention is focused on terrorism rather than the underlying causes that fuel the rightwing militia movement.

If there had been a movement set on violent confrontation with the U.S. government and consisting of 10,000 to 40,000 armed militia members who were African-American, you can bet they would have been investigated months ago, with many members arrested. And you can bet that Congress and the media would have played up the danger.

Beliefs and conspiracy theories

The armed militias are the militant wing of the Patriot movement, which has perhaps five million followers in this country. This diverse rightwing populist movement is composed of independent groups in many states, unified around the idea that the government is increasingly tyrannical. This antigovernment ideology focuses on federal gun control, taxes, regulations, and perceived federal attacks on constitutional liberties.

Many militia members also believe in a variety of conspiracy theories that identify a secret elite that controls the government, the economy, and the culture. Variations on these themes include theories of a secular-humanist conspiracy of liberals to take God out of society, to impose a One World Global Government or a New World Order under the auspices of the United Nations. Though many militia members appear unaware of this, these theories conform to longstanding anti-Semitic ideologies dating to the Nineteenth Century. White-supremacist states'-rights arguments and other theories rooted in racial bigotry also pervade the militia movement.

The Oklahoma bombing was not by any means the first act of public violence with connections to the armed militias.

The Patriot movement is bracketed on the "moderate" side by the John Birch Society and some of Pat Robertson's followers, and on the more militant side by Liberty Lobby and avowedly white-supremacist and anti-Semitic groups, such as neo-Nazi groups. The leadership of preexisting far-right groups, such as the Posse Comitatus, the Aryan Nations, and the Christian Patriots are attempting to steer the armed militia movement toward these white-supremacist and racist ideologies.

Attending a Patriot meeting is like having your cable-access channel video of a PTA meeting crossed with audio from an old *Twilight Zone* rerun. The people seem so sane and regular. They are not clinically deranged, but their discourse is paranoid, and they are awash in the crudest conspiracy theories.

In November 1994, there was a Patriot meeting at a high school in Burlington, Massachusetts, a short distance from Boston and Brookline. Speakers included John Birch Society stalwart Samuel L. Blumenfeld, Sandra Martinez of Concerned Women for America, and leading anti-abortion organizer Dr. Mildred Jefferson. Both the John Birch Society and the Concerned Women for America are also active in the anti-abortion movement.

Jefferson began to speak, tying groups such as NOW [National Organization for Women] and Planned Parenthood to a conspiracy of secular humanists tracing back to the 1800s. Jefferson is a founder and former officer of the National Right to Life committee and a board member of Massachusetts Citizens for Life.

During the meeting, attendees browsed three tables of literature brought by Den's Gun Shop in Lakeville, Massachusetts. One book offered instruction in the use of the Ruger .22 rifle, the weapon used by Salvi. Other books contained diagrams on how to build bombs and incendiary devices. One title was *Improvised Weapons of the American Underground.*

You could even purchase the book *Hunter* by neo-Nazi William Pierce of the National Alliance. *Hunter* is a book about parasitic Jews destroying America, and the need for armed civilians to carry out political assassinations to preserve the white race. Pierce's previous book, *The Turner Diaries*, was the primary sourcebook of racist terror underground organizations, such as The Order, in the 1980s, and still is favored by the neo-Nazi wing of the militias. *The Turner Diaries* includes a section on the bombing of a federal building by the armed underground.

The Turner Diaries *includes a section on the bombing of a federal building by the armed underground.*

One speaker, Ed Brown, runs the Constitutional Defense Militia of New Hampshire. Brown passed out brochures offering "Firearms Training, Combat Leadership, Close Combat, and Intelligence Measures."

The featured afternoon speaker was Robert K. Spear, a key figure in training armed civilian militias. Spear is the author of *Surviving Global Slavery: Living Under the New World Order.* According to Spear, we are living in the "End Times" predicted in the book of Revelations. Spear cited Revelations, Chapter 13, warning that Christians will be asked to accept the Satanic "Mark of the Beast" and reject Christ. True Christians, Spear said, must defend their faith and prepare the way for the return of Christ. Spear believes the formation of armed Christian communities is necessary to prepare for the End Times.

Spear's idea that we are in the End Times is growing in rightwing Christian evangelical circles. While predominantly a Protestant phenomenon, there are small groups of orthodox and charismatic Catholics that also are embracing End Times theology.

These views are hardly marginal within the Christian right. Pat Robertson has been emphasizing this theme on his *700 Club* television program. Just after Christmas 1994, the *700 Club* carried a feature on new dollar-bill designs being discussed to combat counterfeiting. The newscaster then cited Revelations and suggested that if the Treasury Department put new codes on paper money, it might be the Mark of the Beast. Other End Timers believe the Mark of the Beast is hidden in supermarket bar codes or computer microchips.

Rightwing militancy

It is the convergence of various streams of fanatical rightwing beliefs that seems to be sweeping the militia movement along. Overlapping rightwing social movements with militant factions appear to be coalescing within the militias. These include:

• Militant rightwing gun-rights advocates, anti-tax protesters, survivalists, far-right libertarians.

• Preexisting elements of racist, anti-Semitic, or neo-Nazi movements, such as the Posse Comitatus, Christian Identity, or Christian Patriots.

• Advocates of "sovereign" citizenship, "freeman" status, and other arguments rooted in a distorted analysis of the Fourteenth and Fifteenth Amendments. Among this group are those who argue that African Americans are second-class citizens.

• The confrontational wing of the antiabortion movement.

• Apocalyptic millennialists, including some Christians who believe we are in the period of the End Times.

• The dominion theology sector of the Christian evangelical right, especially its most zealous and doctrinaire branch, Christian Reconstructionists.

• The most militant wing of the anti-environmentalist Wise Use movement.

• The most militant wing of the county movement, the Tenth Amendment movement, the states'-rights and the state-sovereignty movements.

This coalescence created a potential for violent assaults against certain targeted scapegoats: federal officials and law-enforcement officers, abortion providers and their pro-choice supporters, environmentalists, people of color, immigrants, welfare recipients, gays and lesbians, and Jews.

Militia-like organizations have existed within the right for many years—in the form of Ku Klux Klan klaverns, the Order cell (out of Aryan Nations), and the Posse Comitatus. But today's citizens' militias, which have sprung up across the country since 1992, represent a new and ominous development within the U.S. rightwing.

But we need to be very careful that we describe the militia phenomenon accurately. Otherwise, we will not blunt the threat, and we may only aid those in this country who are all too eager to curtail our civil liberties.

It would be wrong to assume, as some in the media have, that all members of the armed militias are marginal individuals on the fringes of society.

The first point to underscore about the militias is that not all militia members are racists and anti-Semites. While some militias clearly have emerged, especially in the Pacific Northwest, from old race-hate groups such as the Ku Klux Klan or Aryan Nations, and while the grievances of the militia movement as a whole are rooted in white-supremacist and anti-Semitic conspiracy theories, many militia members do not appear to be consciously drawn to the militia movement on the strength of these issues. Instead, at least consciously, they focus on blaming a caricature of the government for all the specific topical issues that stick in their craw.

To stereotype every armed militia member as a Nazi terrorist not only increases polarization in an already divided nation; it also lumps together persons with unconscious garden-variety prejudice and the demagogues and professional race-hate organizers.

Similarly, it would be wrong to assume, as some in the media have, that all members of the armed militias are marginal individuals on the fringes of society who have no connection to mainstream politics. In this view, there are always a number of fragile people who are subject to political hysteria. When they snap, they adopt an increasingly paranoid style and make militant and unreasonable demands. But this "crackpot" theory is not an accurate picture of everyone in the militia movement; it dismisses out of hand every political grievance they have, and it denies the social roots of the militia movement.

Nor would it be wise to accept the view of the law-enforcement and intelligence agencies, which see the militia movements as the creation of outside agitators who comprise a crafty core of criminal cadre at the epicenter of the movement: These leaders, the theory goes, use the movement as a front to hide their plans for violent armed revolution. Advocates of this view conclude that widespread bugging and infiltration are needed to penetrate to the core of the movement, expose the criminal cadre, and restore order. The larger movement, they claim, will then collapse without the manipulators to urge them to press their grievances, which were never real to begin with.

The problem with these interpretations is that some of the grievances are real.

Social and economic upheaval has fueled militias

We need to remember that the growth of the militias is a social by-product, coming on the heels both of economic hardship and the partial erosion of traditional structures of white male heterosexual privilege. It is at times of economic dislocation and social upheaval that the right has grown dramatically throughout our history. Indeed, the most famous militia movement in the United States, the Ku Klux Klan, arose as a citizens' militia during the turmoil of Reconstruction.

The armed militias are riding the crest of a historically significant rightwing populist revolt in America.

This revolt has arisen from two major stresses: 1) actual economic hardship, caused by global restructuring; and 2) anger over gains by oppressed groups within U.S. society.

Among militia members, there is a great sense of anger over unresolved grievances, over the sense that no one is listening, and this anger has shifted to bitter frustration. The government is perceived to be the enemy because it is the agency by which the economy is governed, and by which equal rights for previously disenfranchised groups are being protected.

But militia members have a point about economic deterioration, and about the systematic expansion of the state's repressive apparatus. These are tenets of populism, which can be participatory and progressive, or scapegoating and regressive.

The last twenty years have seen a decline in real wages for millions of Americans. The farm belt has been particularly hard-hit, and the government shares part of this responsibility, since it urged farmers to borrow heavily and plant fence-to-fence for the Soviet grain deal, then collapsed the farm economy by canceling the deal, which nearly destroyed the family farm.

And the government has abused its power in pursuing and killing rightwing militants without benefit of due process in a series of incidents since 1983, of which Waco was merely the latest and most murderous example.

These wrongs reflect real structures of political and economic inequality central to U.S. policy. Anti-elitism, properly directed, would be a healthy response. But the Patriot movement diverts attention away from actual systems of power by the use of scapegoating and by reducing complex reasons for social and economic conditions to simple formulaic conspiracies.

There is an undercurrent of resentment within the Patriot movement against what are seen as the unfair advantages the government gives to people of color and women through such programs as affirmative action. Thus, the militias are now only the most violent reflection of the backlash against the social-liberation movements of the 1960s and 1970s. The Patriot movement represents an expression of profound anger, virtually a temper tantrum, by a subculture made up primarily, but not exclusively, of white, Christian males.

This temper tantrum is fueled by an old tenet of conspiracy theories: that the country is composed of two types of persons—parasites and producers. The parasites are at the top and the bottom; the producers are the hard-working average citizens in the middle. This analysis lies at the ideological heart of rightwing populism. The parasites at the top are seen as lazy and corrupt government officials in league with wealthy elites who control the currency and the banking sector. The parasites at the bottom are the lazy and shiftless who do not deserve the assistance they receive from society. In the current political scene, this dichotomy between parasites and producers takes on elements of racism because the people at the bottom who are seen as parasites are usually viewed as people of color, primarily black and Hispanic, even though most persons who receive government assistance are white.

The militias are now only the most violent reflection of the backlash against the social-liberation movements of the 1960s and 1970s.

Yet it is not only the angry defense of white male heterosexual privilege that fuels rightwing populism, but also the real economic grievances of working-class and middle-class people. Unless society adapts to address these legitimate grievances, the scapegoating will spread, and rightwing populism can turn to violent authoritarian revolt or move towards fascism.

But even if the society never becomes fascist, the period of turmoil can be dangerous, since it is almost inevitable that someone will conclude that the most efficient solution is to kill the scapegoats.

Responding to militias

How, then, shall we respond to the armed militias? The answer is definitely not to curtail civil liberties. This would serve to further antagonize militia members and reinforce their paranoia about the government. And it would give the government a huge new club to beat up on leftwing dissidents—the typical victims of government repression.

Why should we fear the government? Ask a Japanese American interned during World War II. Ask a member of the American Indian Movement or the Black Panther Party. Ask a Puerto Rican Independence activist. Ask a young African-American male driving through a wealthy suburb. Ask a civil-rights activist. Ask a Vietnam war protester. Ask an anti-interventionist who was monitored by the FBI during its probe of CISPES [Committee in Solidarity with the People of El Salvador] in the 1980s.

When government informants cannot find their suspected terrorists, they have been known to encourage violence where none was planned before their infiltration. This has happened time and again.

Our law-enforcement agencies now manipulate the real presence of fear to demand laws that would undermine freedom of speech. They are once again pursuing the false notion that widespread infiltration can stop the tiny terror cells or violent rebellions that sometimes spin out of dissident social movements when grievances are ignored. Government officials to this day refuse to admit that negligent bureaucratic brutality at Waco could cause any citizen to be distrustful or cynical about government.

Suppressing speech will not solve the problem. But we need to change the tone and content of that speech, which is filled with shrill invective, undocumented assertions, and scapegoating.

The way to disarm the militia movement is to address its real economic grievances, rationally refute its scapegoating, and expose the lies and prejudices that its most fanatical members spew.

Such a strategy was used, with partial success, to confront the Posse Comitatus fifteen years ago. The Posse blamed the collapsing farm economy of the late 1970s and early 1980s on a conspiracy of Jewish bankers manipulating subhuman minorities. In response, a coalition led by the Center for Democratic Renewal in Atlanta organized against scapegoating, offered assistance to groups voicing legitimate economic grievances, and assisted people in reintegrating into the economy.

Teams went county-by-county through Posse strongholds. Black Baptist ministers talked about anti-Semitism; Jews talked about racism; Lutherans talked about healing; farm organizers gave economic advice. The American Jewish Committee hosted a conference in Chicago to call national attention to both anti-Semitism in the farm belt and social and economic injustice in rural America.

This coalition had more to do with beating back the Posse than armed law-enforcement attacks, criminal trials, or civil litigation. What the coalition's education work did not do, however, was uproot the underlying social and economic problems that made the Posse, and now make the Patriot movement, attractive.

The problem is not anger or militancy; . . . the problem is violence.

The widespread rejection of the federal government, and of Democratic and Republican parties alike, points to the need for genuine radical alternatives, which get at the real structures of power and inequality, rather than offering conspiracies and pointing at scapegoats.

The problem is not anger or militancy; the problem is phony answers, the problem is dehumanization, the problem is violence. In 1995, on the fiftieth anniversary of the Nazi Holocaust, it seems troubling to still be debating whether scapegoating can lead to violence and death.

7

Citizen Militias Threaten Democracy

Daniel Junas

Daniel Junas is a Seattle-based political researcher and the author of The Religious Right in Washington State.

The militia movement is gaining support from a growing number of Americans who are frustrated by the federal government, which they perceive as hostile to their interests. This movement—predominantly white, male, and middle or working class—has spread from white supremacist circles to the Christian right. In the western United States, the militia movement's influence has prompted many private landowners and counties to challenge the federal government's environmental regulations and control of public lands. This has led to threats and acts of harassment and violence against federal officials and environmentalists. The eroding of the democratic process caused by the militia movement in these rural areas could easily spread elsewhere.

Winter is harsh in western Montana. Short days, bitter cold and heavy snows enforce the isolation of the small towns and lonely ranches scattered among the broad river valleys and high peaks of the Northern Rockies. But in February 1994—the dead of winter—a wave of fear and paranoia strong enough to persuade Montanans to brave the elements swept through the region. Hundreds of people poured into meetings in small towns to hear tales of mysterious black helicopters sighted throughout the United States and foreign military equipment moving via rail and flatbed truck across the country, in preparation for an invasion by a hostile federal government aided by U.N. troops seeking to impose a New World Order.

In Hamilton (pop. 1,700), at the base of the Bitterroot Mountains dividing Idaho and Montana, 250 people showed up; 200 more gathered in Eureka (pop. 1,000), ten miles from the Canadian border. And 800 people met in Kalispell, at the foot of Glacier National Park. Meeting organizers encouraged their audiences to form citizens' militias to protect

Daniel Junas, "Angry White Guys with Guns: The Rise of the Militias." This article originally appeared in *CovertAction Quarterly*, #52 (Spring 1995), 1500 Massachusetts Ave., #732, Washington, DC 20005; (202) 331-9763. Reprinted with permission.

themselves from the impending military threat.[1]

Most often, John Trochmann, a wiry, white-haired man in his fifties, led the meetings. Trochmann lives near the Idaho border in Noxon (pop. 270), a town well-suited for strategic defense. A one-lane bridge over the Clark Fork River is the only means of access, and a wall of mountains behind the town makes it a natural fortress against invasion. From this bastion, Trochmann, his brother David, and his nephew Randy run the Militia of Montana (MOM), a publicity-seeking outfit that has organized "militia support groups"[2] and pumped out an array of written and taped tales of a sinister global conspiracy controlling the U.S. government. MOM also provides "how to" materials for organizing citizens' militias to meet this dark threat.

Militia mania

It is difficult to judge from attendance at public meetings how many militias and militia members there might be in Montana, or if, as is widely rumored, they are conducting military training and exercises. The same applies across the country; there is little hard information on how many are involved or what they are actually doing.

But the Trochmanns are clearly not alone in raising fears about the federal government nor in sounding the call to arms. By January 1995, movement watchers had identified militia activity in at least 40 states, with a conservatively estimated hard-core membership of at least 10,000—and growing.[3]

The appearance of armed militias raises the level of tension in a region already at war over environmental and land use issues.

A threat explicitly tied to militias occurred in November 1994, at a public hearing in Everett, Washington. Two men approached Ellen Gray, an Audubon Society activist. According to Gray, one of them, later identified as Darryl Lord, placed a hangman's noose on a nearby chair, saying, "This is a message for you." He also distributed cards with a picture of a hangman's noose that said "Treason = Death" on one side, and "Eco fascists go home" on the other. The other man told Gray, "If we can't get you at the ballot box, we'll get you with a bullet. We have a militia of 10,000."[4] In a written statement, Lord later denied making the threat, although he admitted bringing the hangman's noose to the meeting.[5]

The Patriot movement

As important as environmental issues are in the West, they are only part of what is driving the militia movement. The militias have close ties to the older and more broadly based "Patriot" movement, from which they emerged, and which supplies their worldview. According to Chip Berlet, an analyst at Political Research Associates in Cambridge, Massachusetts, who has been tracking the far right for over two decades, this movement consists of loosely-linked organizations and individuals who perceive a global conspiracy in which key political and economic events are manipulated by a small group of elite insiders.

On the far right flank of the Patriot movement are white supremacists and anti-Semites, who believe that the world is controlled by a cabal of Jewish bankers. This position is represented by, among others, the Liberty

Lobby and its weekly newspaper, the *Spotlight*. At the other end of this relatively narrow spectrum is the John Birch Society, which has repeatedly repudiated anti-Semitism, but hews to its own paranoid vision. For the Birchers, it is not the Rothschilds but such institutions as the Council on Foreign Relations, the Trilateral Commission, and the U.N. which secretly call the shots.[6]

This far-right milieu is home to a variety of movements, including Identity Christians, Constitutionalists, tax protesters, and remnants of the semi-secret Posse Comitatus. Members of the Christian right who subscribe to the conspiratorial worldview presented in Pat Robertson's 1991 book, *The New World Order*, also fall within the movement's parameters.[7] Berlet estimates that as many as five million Americans consider themselves Patriots.[8]

While the Patriot movement has long existed on the margins of U.S. society, it has grown markedly in recent years.[9] Three factors have sparked that growth.

One is the end of the Cold War. For over 40 years, the "international communist conspiracy" held plot-minded Americans in thrall. But with the collapse of the Soviet empire, their search for enemies turned toward the federal government, long an object of simmering resentment.

On the far right flank of the Patriot movement are white supremacists and anti-Semites.

The other factors are economic and social. While the Patriot movement provides a pool of potential recruits for the militias, it in turn draws its members from a large and growing number of U.S. citizens disaffected from and alienated by a government that seems indifferent, if not hostile, to their interests. This predominantly white, male, and middle- and working-class sector has been buffeted by global economic restructuring, with its attendant job losses, declining real wages and social dislocations. While under economic stress, this sector has also seen its traditional privileges and status challenged by 1960s-style social movements, such as feminism, minority rights, and environmentalism.

Someone must be to blame. But in the current political context, serious progressive analysis is virtually invisible, while the Patriot movement provides plenty of answers. Unfortunately, they are dangerously wrong-headed ones.[10]

Militias' anti-government sentiment

Two recent events inflamed Patriot passions and precipitated the formation of the militias. The first was the FBI's 1992 confrontation with white supremacist Randy Weaver at Ruby Ridge, Idaho, in which federal agents killed Weaver's son and wife. The second was the federal government's destruction of David Koresh and his followers at the Branch Davidian compound in Waco, Texas, in April 1993.[11] Key promoters of the militia movement repeatedly invoke Ruby Ridge and Waco as spurs to the formation of militias to defend the citizenry against a hostile federal government.

The sense of foreboding and resentment of the federal government was compounded by the passage of the Brady Bill (imposing a waiting period and background checks for the purchase of a handgun) followed by the Crime Bill (banning the sale of certain types of assault rifles). For some members of the Patriot movement, these laws are the federal government's first step in disarming the citizenry, to be followed by the much dreaded United Nations invasion and the imposition of the New World Order.[12]

But while raising apocalyptic fears among Patriots, gun control legislation also angered more mainstream gun owners. Some have become newly receptive to conspiracy theorists and militia recruiters, who justify taking such a radical step with the Second Amendment:

> A well-regulated Militia, being necessary to the security of a free State, the right of the people to keep and bear Arms, shall not be infringed.

Right-wing organizers have long used the amendment to justify the creation of armed formations. The Ku Klux Klan began as a militia movement, and the militia idea has continued to circulate in white supremacist circles. It has also spread within the Christian right. In the early 1990s, the Coalition on Revival, an influential national Christian right networking organization, circulated a 24-plank action plan. It advocated the formation of "a countywide 'well-regulated militia' according to the U.S. Constitution under the control of the county sheriff and Board of Supervisors."[13]

Like the larger Patriot movement, the militias vary in membership and ideology. In the East, they appear closer to the John Birch Society. In New Hampshire, for example, the 15-member Constitution Defense Militia reportedly embraces garden variety U.N. conspiracy fantasies and lobbies against gun control measures.[14] In the Midwest, some militias have close ties to the Christian right, particularly the radical wing of the anti-abortion movement. In Wisconsin, Matthew Trewhella, leader of Missionaries to the Preborn, has organized paramilitary training sessions for his churchmembers.[15]

The militia idea has continued to circulate in white supremacist circles. It has also spread within the Christian right.

And in Indianapolis, Linda Thompson, the self-appointed "Acting Adjutant General of the Unorganized Militia of the U.S.A.," called for an armed march on Washington in September 1994 to demand an investigation of the Waco siege. Although she canceled the march when no one responded, she remains an important militia promoter.[16] While Thompson limits her tirades to U.S. law enforcement and the New World Order, her tactics have prompted the Birch Society to warn its members "to stay clear of her schemes."[17]

Despite slight variations in their motivations, the militias fit within the margins of the Patriot movement. And a recurring theme for all of them is a sense of deep frustration and resentment against the federal government.

Nowhere has that resentment been felt more deeply than in the Rocky Mountain West, a hotbed of such attitudes since the frontier era.

The John Birch Society currently has a larger proportional membership in this region than in any other.[18] Similarly, the Rocky Mountain West is where anti-government presidential candidate Ross Perot ran strongest.

And nowhere in the West is anti-government sentiment stronger than along the spine of wild mountains that divide the Idaho panhandle from Montana. In the last two decades, this pristine setting has become a stomping ground for believers in Christian Identity, a religious doctrine that holds that whites are the true Israelites and that blacks and other people of color are subhuman "mud people."[19]

In the mid-1970s, Richard Butler, a neo-Nazi from California who is carrying out a self-described war against the "Zionist Occupational Government," or "ZOG," relocated to the Idaho panhandle town of Hayden Lake to establish his Aryan Nations compound. He saw the Pacific Northwest, with its relatively low minority population, as the region where God's kingdom could be established. Butler also believed that a racially pure nation needs an army.[20]

Butler is aging, and his organization is mired in factional disputes. But he has helped generate a milieu in which militias can thrive. In May 1992, one of his neighbors and supporters, Eva Vail Lamb, formed the Idaho Organized Militia. During the same year, Lamb was also a key organizer for presidential candidate Bo Gritz (rhymes with "whites"), another key player in the militia movement.[21]

Bo Gritz and the origins of the militias

A former Green Beret, Ret. Lt. Col. Gritz is a would-be Rambo, having led several private missions to Southeast Asia to search for mythical U.S. POWs. He also has a lengthy Patriot pedigree. With well-documented ties to white supremacist leaders, he has asserted that the Federal Reserve is controlled by eight Jewish families.[22] In 1988, he accepted the vice-presidential nomination of the Populist Party an electoral amalgam of neo-Nazis, the Ku Klux Klan, and other racist and anti-Semitic organizations.[23] His running mate was ex-Klansman David Duke. Gritz later disavowed any relationship with Duke, but in 1992, Gritz was back as the Populist Party's candidate for president.

He has emerged as a mentor for the militias. During the 1992 campaign, he encouraged his supporters to form militias,[24] and played a key role in one of the events that eventually sparked the militia movement, the federal assault on the Weaver family compound at Ruby Ridge, Idaho.

In the mid-1980s, Randy Weaver, a machinist from Waterloo, Iowa, moved to Ruby Ridge in Boundary County, the northernmost county in the panhandle. A white supremacist who subscribed to anti-government conspiracy theories, he attended Richard Butler's Aryan Nations congresses at least three times.[25] And acting on the long-held far right notion that the county ought to be the supreme level of government, he even ran for sheriff of Boundary County.

But in 1991, after being arrested on gun charges, Weaver failed to show up for trial and holed up in his mountain home. In August 1992, a belated federal marshals' effort to arrest him led to a siege in which FBI snipers killed Weaver's wife and son, and Weaver associate Kevin Harris killed a federal marshal. Gritz appeared on the scene and interposed himself as a negotiator between the FBI and Weaver. He eventually convinced Weaver to surrender and end the 11-day standoff. The episode gave Gritz national publicity and made him a hero on the right.[26]

He moved quickly to exploit both his newfound fame and the outrage generated by the Weaver killings. In February 1993, Gritz initiated his highly profitable SPIKE training—Specially Prepared Individuals for Key Events. The ten-part traveling program draws on Gritz's Special Forces background and teaches a rigorous course on survival and paramilitary techniques. Gritz—who has already instructed hundreds of Christian Patriots in Oregon, Washington, Idaho, California, and elsewhere—recommends the training as essential preparation for militia members.[27]

The Randy Weaver shootout also led directly to the formation of the Trochmanns' Militia of Montana (MOM). In September 1992, during the Ruby Ridge standoff, John Trochmann helped found United Citizens for Justice (UCJ), a support group for his friend Weaver. Another steering committee member was Chris Temple, who writes regularly for the *Jubilee*, a leading Christian Identity publication. Temple also worked as a western Montana organizer for Gritz's presidential campaign. One of the earliest mailing lists used to promote MOM came from UCJ.

Catron was the first county to issue a direct legal challenge to the federal government over [public] lands.

But despite Trochmann's links to their adherents, white supremacist and Christian Identity rhetoric is conspicuously absent from MOM literature.[28] Instead, Trochmann purveys the popular U.N./New World Order conspiracy theory with an anti-corporate twist. The cabal, he claims, intends to reduce the world's population to two billion by the year 2000.[29]

At public events, he cites news accounts, government documents and reports from his informal intelligence network. Trochmann also reports on the mysterious black helicopters and ties them to the U.N. takeover plot. In one of his lectures, distributed on a MOM videotape, he uses as evidence a map—found on the back of a Kix cereal box—which divides the United States into ten regions, reflecting, he implies, an actual plan to divide and conquer the nation.[30]

The Trochmanns give talks around the country and are part of a very effective alternative media network which uses direct mail, faxes, videos, talk radio, TV, and even computers linked to the Internet to sustain its apocalyptic, paranoid worldview.[31]

The Trochmanns use all these venues to promote MOM materials, including an organizing manual, "Militia Support Group," which provides a model military structure for the militias and lays out MOM's aims:

> The time has come to renew our commitment to high moral values and wrench the control of the government from the hands of the secular humanists and the self-indulging special interest groups including private corporations.[32]

It also reveals that MOM has recruited "Militia Support Groups" throughout the nation into its intelligence network, which provides

MOM with a steady stream of information to feed into its conspiracy theories. Consequently, the Trochmanns were well aware when trouble was brewing in another remote corner of the West.

The County Rule movement

In Catron County, New Mexico, the militia movement has converged with some other strands of the anti-government right to create a new challenge to federal power. Catron, located in the desolate southwest of New Mexico and with a population of less than 3,000 people, has been the site of a novel legal challenge to federal control of public lands. In what has become known as the County Rule movement, Catron was the first county to issue a direct legal challenge to the federal government over those lands.

It grew out of a conflict between local ranchers and federal land managers over federal grazing lands. County attorney James Catron, whose ancestors gave the county its name, joined forces with Wyoming attorney Karen Budd, a long-time foe of environmental regulation,[33] to produce the Catron County ordinances. These purport to give the county ultimate authority over public lands—making it illegal for the U.S. Forest Service to regulate grazing, even on its own lands.[34]

But such regulations also serve the interests of natural resource industries. Since it is relatively easy for those industries to control county governments, the ordinances provide them with a convenient end run around federal environmental laws and rules. The Catron County legislation has since been disseminated throughout the West—and recently into the Midwest—by the National Federal Lands Conference of Bountiful, Utah, which is part of the anti-environmental Wise Use movement.[35]

Over 100 counties in the West have passed similar legislation, despite the ordinances' shaky legal foundations. The Boundary County, Idaho, ordinances have been overturned in state court, and federal court challenges to county rule legislation in Washington state are expected to succeed; the U.S. Supreme Court has consistently upheld federal government authority over federal lands.[36]

Nevertheless, the County Rule movement has succeeded in shifting the balance of power between the counties and the federal government, if through no other means than intimidation. In Catron County, the sheriff has threatened to arrest the head of the local Forest Service office. And the county also passed a resolution predicting "much physical violence" if the federal government persists in trying to implement grazing reform.[37]

Militias do not pose a military threat to the federal government. But they do threaten democracy.

In fact, a climate of hostility greets environmentalists throughout the West. Author David Helvarg writes that there have been hundreds of instances of harassment and physical violence in the last few years.[38] Sheila O'Donnell, a California-based private investigator who tracks harassment of environmentalists, concurs that intimidation is on the rise.[39]

Catron County has been the scene of at least one such incident.

Richard Manning, a local rancher, planned to open a mill at the Challenger mine, on Forest Service land in the Mogollon mountains. Forest Service and state regulators want to determine if toxic mine tailings are leaching into watercourses. According to several Forest Service and state officials, Manning threatened to meet any regulator with "a hundred men with rifles." Manning denies having made the threat.⁴⁰

The County Rule movement and the militias share an ideological kinship, revolving around the idea, long popular in far-right circles, that the county is the supreme level of government and the sheriff the highest elected official. "Posse Comitatus"—the name for a far-right, semi-secret anti-tax organization—literally means "the power of the county."

A militia has formed in Catron County, quickly sparking an incident that demonstrates the high level of paranoia in the area. In September 1994, two days after the militia held its first meeting, FBI and National Guard officials arrived in Catron County to search for the body of a person reportedly killed a year earlier in the nearby Mogollon mountains. Several militia members refused to believe the official explanation and fled their homes for the evening.⁴¹

Catron County may be a bellwether: The County Rule and militia movements are apparently converging. In October 1994, the monthly newsletter of the National Federal Lands Conference featured a lead article that explicitly called for the formation of militias. The article, which cited information provided by the Militia of Montana and pro-militia organizations in Idaho and Arizona, closed by saying:

> At no time in our history since the colonies declared their independence from the long train of abuses of King George has our country needed a network of active militias across America to protect us from the monster we have allowed our federal government to become. Long live the Militia! Long live freedom! Long live government that fear [sic] the people!⁴²

Such incendiary rhetoric, commonplace in the Patriot/Militia movement, makes an armed confrontation between the government and militia members seem increasingly likely. If past behavior is any guide, federal law enforcement agencies are all too ready to fight fire with fire.

Obviously, militias do not pose a military threat to the federal government. But they do threaten democracy. Armed militias fueled by paranoid conspiracy theories could make the democratic process unworkable, and in some rural areas of the West, it is already under siege.

As ominously, the militias represent a smoldering right-wing populism—with real and imagined grievances stoked by a politics of resentment and scapegoating—just a demagogue away from kindling an American fascist movement.

The militia movement now is like a brush fire on a hot summer day, atop a high and dry mountain ridge on the Idaho panhandle. As anyone in the panhandle can tell you, those brush fires have a way of getting out of control.

Notes

1. Montana Human Rights Network, "A Season of Discontent: Militias, Constitutionalists, and The Far Right in Montana," May 1994.

2. Paramilitary formations are illegal in Montana. Militia organizers skirt the law by forming "support groups."

3. Interview with Chip Berlet, Dec. 21, 1994.

4. Diane Brooks, "Threats Replace Debate at Hearing," *Seattle Times*, Snohomish edition, Nov. 15, 1994, p. B1; interview with Ellen Gray by Paul de Armond, Nov. 22, 1994.

5. Statement to the press, Nov. 16, 1994.

6. For Birch Society theories, see its magazine, *The New American*; also James Perloff, *The Council on Foreign Relations and the American Decline* (Belmont, Mass.: Western Islands, 1988), and Dan Smoot, *The Invisible Government* (Belmont, Mass.: Western Islands, 1965).

7. Pat Robertson, *The New World Order* (Irving, Tex.: New Publishers, 1991).

8. Berlet interview, *op. cit.*

9. *Ibid.* Berlet notes that the John Birch Society has rebounded from a low of 20,000 members and claims to have doubled its membership in recent years. Berlet believes membership has probably increased by 10,000.

10. This analysis is based on interviews with long-time movement watcher Chip Berlet, Feb. 6, 1995.

11. The behavior of federal law enforcement agencies merits criticism. Weaver and actual shooter Kevin Harris were acquitted of murder charges in the death of a federal agent during the siege. A December 1993 Justice Department report on the Weaver standoff found that FBI agents violated both bureau policies and constitutional guidelines when they issued "rules of engagement" allowing agents to shoot any armed adult. [As of early 1995] an Idaho prosecutor's investigation continued, and FBI head Louis Freeh expected two agents to be indicted. (Jerry Seper, "Probe of federal agents in siege killings continues," *Washington Times*, Feb. 13, 1995, p. A3). Similarly, the Justice Department's *Report to the Deputy Attorney General on the Events at Waco, Texas, February 28 to April 19, 1993* faulted BATF and FBI performance, but found no cause for indictments.

12. See "Under the Law of the Gun," *Taking Aim* (Militia of Montana newsletter), v. 1, n. 7, 1994, pp. 1–3.

13. Fred Clarkson, "HardCOR," *Church and State*, Jan. 1991, p. 26.

14. Anti-Defamation League, *Armed and Dangerous: Militias Take Aim at the Federal Government*, 1994, p. 20.

15. John Goetz, "Missionaries' Leader Calls for Armed Militia," *Front Line Research*, Aug. 1994, pp. 1, 3–4; Beth Hawkins, "Patriot Games," *Metro Times* (Detroit), Oct. 12–18, 1994, pp. 12–16.

16. Adam Parfrey and Jim Redden, "Patriot Games," *Village Voice*, Oct. 11, 1994, pp. 26–31.

17. Cited in Anti-Defamation League, *op. cit.*, p. 12.

18. Charles Jeffrey Kraft, "A Preliminary Socio-Economic and State Demographic Profile of the John Birch Society," Political Research Associates, 1991.

19. Leonard Zeskind, "The 'Christian Identity' Movement," National Council of Churches, 1986.

20. In 1984, Butler's vision briefly materialized in the form of an Aryan Nations offshoot led by Robert Jay Matthews. The Order committed a series of crimes, including bank robberies, bombings, and the murder of Denver radio talk show host Alan Berg. Matthews himself died in a shootout with police in December 1984 on Whidbey Island, in Puget Sound near Seattle. See Robert Crawford, S.L. Gardiner, Jonathan Mozzochi, and R.L. Taylor, *The Northwest Imperative* (Portland, Ore.: Coalition for Human Dignity, 1994), p. 1.16.

21. Robert Crawford, S.L. Gardiner, Jonathan Mozzochi, "Patriot Games," Coalition for Human Dignity Special Report, 1994.

22. Crawford, *et al.*, *Northwest Imperative, op. cit.*, p. 2.25; Gritz nonetheless denies that he is a white supremacist. Phone interview by David Neiwert, Nov. 10, 1994.

23. Crawford, *et al.*, *Northwest Imperative*, p. 1.32.

24. Montana Human Rights Network, *op. cit.*, p. 7

25. Philip Weiss, "Off the Grid," *New York Times Magazine*, Jan. 8, 1995, pp. 24–33.

26. Weiss, *op. cit.*; Crawford, *et al.*, *Northwest Imperative, op. cit.*, p. 2.27.

27. Phone interview by David Neiwert, *op. cit.*

28. Trochmann denies being a white supremacist. In 1990, however, he was a featured speaker at an Aryan Nations congress and has since admitted travelling to the white supremacist compound on at least four or five occasions. Interview by David Neiwert, Nov. 15, 1994.

29. *Ibid.*

30. *Militia of Montana Information Video and Intel Update*, videotape, undated.

31. Interview with Ken Toole, president, Montana Human Rights Network, Jan. 9, 1995; Anti-Defamation League, "Armed and Dangerous: Militias Take Aim at the Federal Government," 1994, pp. 7–9.

32. Militia of Montana, "Militia Support Group," undated.

33. Budd formerly worked for James Watt in the Interior Dept., as well as for Watt's former employer, the anti-environment, corporate-funded Mountain States Legal Foundation. Barry Sims, "Private rights in public lands?" *The Workbook* (Albuquerque), Summer 1993, p. 55.

34. Charles McCoy, "Catron County, N.M. Leads a Nasty Revolt Over Eco-Protection," *Wall Street Journal*, Jan. 3, 1995; Scott Reed, "The County Supremacy Myth: Mendacious Myth Marketing," *Idaho Law Review*, v. 30, 1994, pp. 526–53; interview with Tarso Ramos, Western States Center, Dec. 21, 1994.

35. The "Wise Use" movement has recently emerged as a potent political force in the West. It is largely the brainchild of Ron Arnold, who has been helping logging, mining, and agricultural corporations fight the environmental movement since the mid-1970s. Since 1985 Arnold has headed the corporate-funded Center for the Defense of Free Enterprise (CDFE), controlled by Alan Gottlieb, a New Right direct mail fundraiser best known for his opposition to gun control. See Alan Gottlieb, ed., *The Wise Use Agenda* (Bellevue, Wash.: Free Enterprise Press, 1989). The National Federal Lands Conference supported the first Wise Use conference. See National Federal Lands Conference brochure, 1994.

36. McCoy, *op. cit.*

37. *Ibid.*

38. David Helvarg, *The War Against the Greens* (San Francisco: Sierra Club Books, 1994), p. 326.

39. Interview, Jan. 9, 1995.

40. McCoy, *op. cit.*

41. Tony Davis, "Militia Members scatter as FBI, Guard turn up in Catron," *Albuquerque Tribune*, Sept. 14, 1994.

42. Jim Faulkner, "Why There is a Need for the Militia in America," *Update*, National Federal Lands Conference, October 1994.

8

The Militia Movement Is Misguided

Karen L. MacNutt

Karen L. MacNutt is a Boston attorney and a rifle and pistol competitor. She is also a consultant for the Second Amendment Foundation, the National Rifle Association, and Gun Owners Action League, all organizations that advocate the right of individuals to own guns.

The only legal role of militias is as groups of citizens that form part of the military and take orders from federal, state, and local governments. It is unlawful for private militia groups to take action simply to promote their policies. Militias that act independently are unwittingly setting themselves up as scapegoats for a government that is intent on seeking an enemy to exploit. Their actions are giving government an excuse to try to restrict individual ownership of guns and other rights. Militia members are wasting valuable resources by trying to achieve their political goals in this manner. Instead, they should focus their efforts on the electoral process.

A growing number of Americans have been attracted to the so-called "militia" movement. By that I am not talking about historical re-enactments, the National Guard, or any organization sponsored by a local or state government. I am not talking about military schools, survivalists, self-defense courses or adventure game people.

I am talking about those who have joined private associations which they believe constitute the "militia" of the United States. For the most part they are good-hearted, honest, well-meaning, loyal but naive Americans who are legitimately concerned over our increasing loss of individual freedom, loss of nationality, and the growth of violent, politically inspired, law enforcement activity.

These are serious concerns which must be met with effective action; action which the American public has the power to implement through the ballot box.

Those who believe they can preserve American freedoms through the

Karen L. MacNutt, "Militias: Training for Doomsday . . . or Feeding Anti-gun Strategists?" *Gun News Digest*, Summer 1995. Reprinted by permission of the author.

"militia" movement are sadly mistaken.

The "militia" movement is flawed. It has failed to properly define the strategic centers of power of those they claim to oppose. That center of power is not the military. It is public opinion. Because they have not properly defined the problem, the "militia" movement is playing into the hands of the very people it fears.

America's most dangerous enemy is its own imagination run wild. There is an epidemic of people convinced that our world or society is coming to an end for one reason or the other. They say something horrible will happen unless drastic steps are taken. Their fears will become a self-fulfilling prophesy unless people stop looking at our society as a place where the tyranny of the majority forces its concept of "good" on its neighbors.

On one side of this growing epidemic are people who see big government and internationalists as the destroyers of freedom. They see "foreign troops" in the United States as evidence that the end of our sovereignty is near.

Unfounded fears

I may well believe that big government and internationalists are a threat to American freedom. I may well believe America's progression towards fascism, a form of socialism that allows individuals to hold title to property but gives control to the government, is far progressed. But fears based on the sighting of foreign troops in the United States are not well founded and do not address the real problem. Foreign troops have trained in the United States for over 50 years. Joint exercises have been held in the United States and in other nations since the Second World War. There is nothing new or evil about this. Because the US contributes to UN "peacekeeping" missions, UN marked vehicles will turn up on US military reservations. Often these are our own vehicles which have not been repainted after a UN mission. Since the Gulf War, Soviet-made vehicles have shown up on military reservations to increase training realism or as war trophies. There is nothing evil about that either.

Commentators who use such things to scare the American public are so far off base that they discredit those who are seriously concerned about the path our country has taken. Such claims are provocative and will eventually lead some well meaning American to do something really dumb. When that occurs, those who are our true enemies will use the incident to abrogate more of our liberties and take more power for themselves.

On the other side of the equation are all those agencies that must justify their budgets to Congress every year. At one time they had Russian spies to watch. Now they have to find a new "threat" to justify their existence.

These agencies and TV journalists have something in common. They would both be out of a job if they reported the truth; that is, on some days absolutely nothing newsworthy happens. The journalists, like the agencies, must find a "problem" to justify their jobs. They will strain to find illegal activity even if they have to create it. There is no "conspiracy" to all this, just human greed.

Those of you who followed the Randy Weaver incident in Idaho will remember what led federal agents to besieging Weaver's wilderness home. It was Weaver's refusal to help agents obtain incriminating information on the "politically incorrect" groups he belonged to or had access to. Well, I disapprove of those groups; but under our system of government they have a right to exist without government agents twisting the law to prosecute them. Weaver claimed that federal agents altered a gun after Weaver sold it to them in an attempt to blackmail Weaver. The agents claimed the gun was illegal. Weaver refused to turn informant. What next occurred had all the earmarks of a Mafia hit. When Weaver missed a court date on the gun charge, US Marshals surrounded Weaver's home and, in the ensuing gun fight, killed his 14-year-old son and, in the standoff which followed, an FBI sniper killed Weaver's unarmed wife while she was holding an infant. Some believe that had it not been for the persistence of Weaver's friends, the agents would have killed everyone in the Weaver household. No satisfactory legal action has been taken against the agents. Although this might sound preposterous, it tracks federal law enforcement tactics when those tactics are played to extreme ends.

The methods used by federal law enforcement against drug dealers have been: the sting, where government agents set up an illegal situation to see if the person targeted will commit a crime; or the informant, where someone is given immunity or leniency for an offense if they will testify against others. With only a slight twist, these methods can become an illegal entrapment or extortion.

Fears based on the sighting of foreign troops in the United States are not well founded.

It is chilling to watch our "elite" hunt around for someone to use as a scapegoat to justify their failed policies and continuous grasp for power. Innocuous groups and practices are given sinister appearances. Even religion is being targeted. Small religious groups are called "cults" to be feared by the public and ridiculed by the government. Large religious groups are said to "interfere" with government in violation of the "separation" clause of the Constitution because they criticize the elite or oppose a fashionable immorality.

The business of religion is to speak against immorality. They do not violate the "separation" clause because there is no "separation of church and state" clause in the Constitution. The Constitution prohibits Congress from establishing a religion and it prohibits Congress from preventing people from exercising their own religion.

Looking for an "enemy"

If religion is being set up for persecution, then the "militias" do not stand a chance. What our new "politically correct elite" preaches is pure prejudice. The type of prejudice that led federal agents to commit the crime of genocide at Waco, Texas, where federal agents destroyed an entire religious sect. Key to that destruction was a successful propaganda campaign designed to isolate the Branch Davidians from their natural allies, law-abiding gunowners and the religious communities.

At the very time the government is looking for an "enemy" to "guard" the public against, good citizens are being convinced to dress up in military style clothes and look very menacing to their neighbors. They are doing this in the face of a concerted, and partially successful, campaign by the anti-gun forces to make anything "military" seem evil unless controlled by the government. Indeed, high on the anti-gun agenda is the objective to suppress anything that promotes a "culture of violence." They are, in short, not interested in crime; they want to legislate against ideas. They are book burners at heart.

Not only is the "militia" movement playing into the hands of its enemies, its philosophy is flawed.

The "militias" are perfect targets for those who need an "enemy" to "investigate." The private "militias" look and sound menacing. They possess things many people fear. When the time comes for the government to move against such groups, they will find themselves isolated from the general public. They will be made to look like such fanatics that no one will question the repressive acts of the government. No one will come to their defense. The publicity will be so bad, even their friends will abandon them out of fear of being dragged down.

Those in the "militia" movement might as well have uniforms with bullseyes painted on them and a big sign that says "kick me." Their organizations will ultimately provide the excuse for government to enact all sorts of restrictive legislation not only against guns, but against the civilian ownership or knowledge of anything the government defines as "military." After all, the elitists will say, what legitimate sporting need is there for civilians to have military equipment?

Not only is the "militia" movement playing into the hands of its enemies, its philosophy is flawed.

The "militia" movement is based on a premise the anti-gun groups have pushed for years, that the Second Amendment is a collective right and only the "militia" is guaranteed the fight to have arms.

That is absolutely false. The Second Amendment is an individual right. The Constitution is a compact or contract between equals. Those equals are each individual American. The founders of our country believed that everyone had the God-given right to determine what was in his or her own interest. No individual was better, or had a higher right by reason of birth or position than any other individual. Government was the creation of the people and existed to defend the rights of the individuals. The "People" of the Constitution are the individual people of the original states who voted to adopt the Constitution. All Americans today are the heirs to their legacy.

Throughout the Constitution, the word "People" means the individual citizen. Look at the Fourth Amendment which states:

> The right of the people to be secure in their persons, houses, papers, and effects, against unreasonable searches and seizures, shall not be violated. . . .

No one would seriously claim the Fourth Amendment was not an individual right. When the Constitution talked of collective rights, it spoke in terms of the states such as in Section 10 of the Constitution which states:

> No State shall, without the consent of Congress . . . keep troops or ships of War in times of Peace. . . .

The anti-gun forces say that only the militia can have guns. It is clear that Congress has full control over the militia of the Constitution. Under Section 10 of the Constitution, Congress could abolish the National Guard or, as it is currently doing, reduce it to any size it wished.

Section 9 of the Constitution gives the federal government the power:

> To provide for the organizing, arming, and disciplining, of the Militia, and for governing such part of them as may be employed in the Service of the United States, reserving to the States respectively, the appointment of the officers, and authority of training the Militia according to the discipline prescribed by Congress.

The Constitution gives the federal government control over all the military forces of the United States including the militia.

Militias: beholden to government

But what is this Militia? The Militia was, and still is, a grouping of citizens capable of being called to military service. It is not an organization. Individuals in the group have no power to act unless they are called to service. Once mustered into service, the militiaman becomes part of the military and is placed in a military unit. He is subject to military law and is obliged to obey the orders of his officers.

Who has the power to call out the militia? The President, your Governor, and in most states, the sheriff or the municipal authorities. The purpose for which the militia can be called into service is to enforce the law, to protect the lives and property of the citizens of the community, to suppress riot or insurrection, or to repel invasion.

The promotion of policy or politics is not a lawful reason to call forth the militia. When the militiaman becomes a soldier, he loses his right to trial by jury and can be punished by a court martial, a board of military officers. If he fails to obey the lawful orders of his superiors, he can be punished. In time of war, he can be executed for failure to obey those orders. If a group of militiamen fail to obey orders, and engage in what would be considered lawful protest in the civilian world, the military considers that mutiny. Mutiny is a serious offense which, under certain conditions, can be punished by death. If a body of persons under arms resists the lawful orders of civilian authorities, that may equal sedition or treason. Those crimes also carry the death penalty.

Being in an active militia unit is not a game. It carries legal responsibilities.

Although America has had a long history of "independent" militia companies, those companies were always chartered and sanctioned by the civil authority. After the American Revolution, independent militia companies became fashionable just as did fraternal organizations such as the Masons. The companies often had fanciful names and uniforms patterned after some elite European unit. If you are ever in Boston on the first Monday in June, go to Boston Common. There you will witness the election of officers of the Ancient and Honorable Artillery Company, the nation's oldest militia group. The pageantry is outstanding.

The independent militia companies were chartered by the states, swore allegiance to the state, and were a part of the state's military forces. They were only "independent" in that they were not part of the rigid county militia companies required by the early militia laws. The "independent" companies were subject to being incorporated into the active army during times of emergency. Indeed, they were, in large measure, the people who fought our Civil War.

The farmers who fought the British at Concord and Lexington in 1775 all signed the muster book and were soldiers at the time of the battle. The state payroll still exists for their services. They were not a mob or private association. They were the agents of municipal and county government instructed to enforce local law and protect local citizens.

What was important about Concord and Lexington was that local government committed itself to the side of American Independence.

As long as the civilian authority is elected by the people, it represents the wishes of the people. To maintain the Republic, all armed forces must be answerable to the people through their elected representatives.

No matter how much you may disagree with elected officials, our system of government gives them the authority to control the military. It reserves to the people the right to get rid of those officials through elections. It also reserves to the individual people the right to keep and bear arms to defend themselves and their rights. The resort to force, however, is never justified while we have the ability to elect our government and conduct our affairs under the rule of law.

The reason the Second Amendment guarantees individual people the right to keep and bear arms, not the militia companies, is that there was a fear that the federal government would use its power to equip and call the militia to duty as a means to disarm the general population. It was therefore necessary that individuals, in their individual capacity, not their military capacity, have the right to have guns.

The authors of the Constitution believed in universal military training. They were adamantly opposed to leaving matters of arms in the hands of professionals. In looking to the historical precedents and the writings of [Italian statesman and philosopher] Niccolò Machiavelli, they believed the greatest threat to a republic was a professional armed force, be it the army or an internal security force.

> *The promotion of policy or politics is not a lawful reason to call forth the militia.*

The authors of the Constitution felt that if the whole population were trained to arms and were in fact armed, no one would dare try to overthrow the Republic. What they established was a balance of power much like the Mutually Assured Destruction concept which prevented a nuclear war during the Cold War. It was not that an armed population would have an easy time forcing a rogue army to behave, but the resulting civil war would be long, bloody, and as destructive as anything we have seen in Lebanon, the Balkans or Africa. It was an assurance that no one could profit from an attempt to seize power. It was not a preferred form of action. It was a result so terrible that no one would wish to risk the event.

Popular support eclipses military might

It has been a long while since there was a land-based war in the United States. If such a war took place, our cities would look just as devastated as those in Bosnia. Our children would be just as pathetic. Our population would starve just as readily. It is not an undertaking that any sane person would willingly engage in.

America has a long tradition of the military keeping out of politics. We have avoided the military coups which have plagued many other countries by acknowledging a simple truth that the "militia" movement ignores. As revolutionaries from Sam Adams to Mao Zedong will tell you, you cannot have a successful revolution without the support of the people. As any military authority will tell you, you cannot win a war unless you have a well disciplined force and the organization to supply it. In our system of government, if you are well organized and have the support of the people, you do not need violence to control the government. You just make sure your supporters vote.

Our Constitution is a marvelous document which institutionalized revolution. Within its pages, it provides for the peaceful overthrow of the government every two to six years through the electoral process.

We have witnessed such a revolution. The Republicans captured Congress [in the November 1994 election] because they were better organized and had more public support than the Democrats.

The Second Amendment guarantees individual people the right to keep and bear arms, not the militia companies.

Unlike some nations, the shift of power in the United States was so orderly that most people were unaware of the amount of power that changed hands. In 1996, the "revolution" of 1994 will either continue or be lost when the President runs for office. A continuation of the "revolution" could result in the continued control of the House of Representatives, up to two thirds of the Senate, and the Presidency. Control of the Senate and Presidency leads to the control of the Supreme Court. Politically savvy power brokers are already marshaling their "troops" for that fight.

While some Americans are running around the woods training for a doomsday that will not arrive in the way they envision, real power is being amassed by those who create and control the political machines which make and break candidates. The glory of the American system is that anyone can build a machine.

As long as the American people can vote and run for office, the method the Constitution provides for righting political wrongs is through the political campaign. If we have bad government, it is because too many good people do not pay attention to the political system. From time to time, the people will rise up to vent their anger in an election. Our job is to keep that political pressure on.

That brings us back to the "militia."

There is a big difference in being a part of *the* militia and being part of *a* militia. *The* militia are all citizens capable of bearing arms. *A* militia is an organization of citizen soldiers. I have no problem with such organizations when organized by a city, county or state, but I do have problems with private militias.

Where the regular army is the military power of the central government, the militia is the military power of county and municipal governments. The militia companies were a part of local government. Just as people elected their selectmen, the militia companies often elected their own officers.

Until World War I every time the United States went to war it had to ask the states for the troops to wage war as the regular army was not large enough to do so on its own. This method insured that any commitment of our armed forces would be publicly approved. The first time we attempted to wage a major war without such approval was Korea. The second time was Vietnam.

The American military, including the militia, have a long, honorable and good tradition of not being political. The Constitution places the military under the control of civilian authorities elected by, and responsible to, the people. That is as it should be.

Real militiamen are subject to military discipline under the UCMJ [Uniform Code of Military Justice] or the equivalent state militia law. They can be punished if they engage in conduct that is inappropriate for a soldier, even if that conduct would be lawful for a civilian.

The private "militia" companies are implicitly accepting the anti-gun argument that the Second Amendment does not guarantee individuals the right to keep and bear arms. The Second Amendment is an individual right. The right exists so that the people can defend themselves individually and be available when called by the civil authority to enforce the laws or defend the community from invasion. If the Second Amendment referred to militias, then arguably only those people in an organization controlled by the government would be able to have guns.

Effective political action

By running around in "militia" companies, people are wasting valuable resources which could be used for effective political action. Our opponents are using the political system for all it is worth. We need every man and woman working in the trenches of political campaigns, not in the woods. We can affect elections. We can be politically powerful. The November 1994 elections show that. We must keep up the political pressure. If the organizational time and ability being used to create "militias" were used to create effective political machines, we would control numerous elections.

Real soldiering is not fun. It is grueling, tedious grunt work interspersed with moments of abject terror and hideous destruction. Political campaigning is tiring, monotonous work interspersed with raucous parties and wild rallies. Parties are more fun than devastation.

Last, the anti-gun factions have historically made progress by frightening the American public. The "assault weapon" legislation [banning many types of semiautomatic weapons in 1994] passed because of the panic created in the general population. We have entered an era when much of the security forces of the federal government need to create a "threat" to justify their appropriations. Agency rumblings about "cults," "survivalists," "right wing extremisms," and "neo-Nazis" are all warning signs that there will be an attempt to create the image of an internal enemy to justify budgets and the repression of political opponents. The only "fascists" we have to worry about are those who hold high government office and attempt to justify destroying individual rights in the name of some collective "good."

By running around in "militia" companies, people are wasting valuable resources which could be used for effective political action.

The "militia" groups play into the hands of our enemies. Some flashy crime will occur and rightly or wrongly the "militia" groups will be blamed. There will be exposés on the tabloid TV programs guaranteed to make all gunowners look crazy. There will be a demand for Congress to act. No elected official will want to be seen with radicals even though they will privately admit there is nothing to all the media hype. Legislation outlawing all sorts of things will be pushed through outlawing things that promote what the anti-gunners call "the culture of violence." That includes historical reenactments, the collecting of military memorabilia, the right of self-defense, and the thought that individuals can make up their own minds as to what is in their own best interests. It will all be illegal because what the elitists want to control is our beliefs, not our actions.

The key to preserving freedom is to educate the American public, to organize for effective political action, and to use our organizational resources to take advantage of the political process to its fullest.

Organizations to Contact

The editors have compiled the following list of organizations concerned with the issues debated in this book. The descriptions are derived from materials provided by the organizations. All have publications or information available for interested readers. The list was compiled on the date of publication of the present volume; names, addresses, phone and fax numbers, and e-mail/internet addresses may change. Be aware that many organizations take several weeks or longer to respond to inquiries, so allow as much time as possible.

America's Promise Ministries (APM)
PO Box 157
Sandpoint, ID 83864
(208) 265-5405
fax: (208) 265-5415

America's Promise is a nondenominational ministry that believes that "Anglo-Saxons are the true descendants of the house of Israel." It believes that the United States is no longer the Christian society it once was and that individuals' freedom and liberty are being threatened by a hostile government. APM publishes the monthly *America's Promise Newsletter*.

Anti-Defamation League (ADL)
823 United Nations Plaza
New York, NY 10017
(212) 490-2525
fax: (212) 867-0779

ADL works to stop the defamation of Jews and to ensure fair treatment for all U.S. citizens. It advocates state and federal governments' adoption of penalty-enhancement laws and antiparamilitary training statutes as a means to fight hate crimes. It publishes the quarterly *Facts* magazine and distributes reports such as "Armed and Dangerous: Militias Take Aim at the Federal Government" and "Beyond the Bombing: The Militia Menace Grows."

Center for Action for the Center for Patriotic Activity
c/o HC 11 Box 307
Kamiah, ID 83536
(208) 935-2918
fax: (208) 935-2739
internet: http://www.bogritz.com

Created in 1989 by Bo Gritz, a former Green Beret, the center is dedicated to protecting Americans' constitutional rights and promoting survival and self-preparedness techniques. It publishes the monthly *Center for Action Newsletter*, which focuses on current events, both within the United States and throughout the world, and how these events may affect Americans' freedom and security.

Center to Prevent Handgun Violence
1225 Eye St. NW, Rm. 1100
Washington, DC 20005
(202) 289-7319
fax: (202) 408-1851

The center works to reduce gun violence through education, research, and legal advocacy. The center's Legal Action Project represents gun-violence victims in liability suits, defends gun-control laws under attack in the courts, and fosters public understanding of the legal issues bearing on society's response to gun violence. The center publishes the booklet *The Second Amendment: Myth and Meaning.*

Citizens Committee for the Right to Keep and Bear Arms
12500 NE Tenth Pl.
Bellevue, WA 98005
(206) 454-4911
fax: (206) 451-3959

The committee believes that the U.S. Constitution's Second Amendment guarantees and protects the right of individual Americans to own guns. It works to educate the public concerning this right and to lobby legislators to prevent the passage of gun-control laws. The committee is affiliated with the **Second Amendment Foundation** and has more than six hundred thousand members. It publishes the books *Gun Laws of America, Gun Rights Fact Book, Origin of the Second Amendment,* and *Point Blank.*

Coalition for Human Dignity (CHD)
PO Box 21266
Seattle, WA 98111-3266
(206) 233-9775
fax: (206) 233-9850

CHD monitors the far right and works against bigotry. It publishes the reports "Against the New World Order: The American Militia Movement," "The Northwest Imperative: Documenting a Decade of Hate," and "Guns and Gavels: Common Law Courts, Militias, and White Supremacy."

The Free American
PO Box 2943
Bingham, NM 87832
(505) 423-3250
fax: (505) 423-3258
e-mail: freeamerican@etsc.net

The Free American is committed to restoring the U.S. Constitution and exposing communism, corruption, and crime. It objects to media assertions that the Patriot movement is antigovernment. Group members oppose corrupt government officials, traitors, and government-sponsored terrorism. Its publications include the monthly tabloid *Free American* and the books *Constitution: Fact or Fiction?* and *Restoring America: The Second American Revolution.*

The Lawyer's Second Amendment Society
18034 Ventura Blvd., #329
Encino, CA 91316
(818) 734-3066
internet: rkbaesq@ix.netcom.com

The society is a nationwide network of attorneys and others who are interested in preserving the right to keep and bear arms. It attempts to educate citizens about what it believes is their inalienable right, provided by the Constitution's framers, to defend themselves with firearms if necessary. The society publishes the *Liberty Poll* newsletter six times a year.

Militia of Montana (MOM)
PO Box 1486
Noxon, MT 59853
(406) 847-2735
fax: (406) 847-2246

MOM is an educational enterprise dedicated to picking up where the mainstream media have left off informing the public. It believes that the mainstream media are not doing their job because they are keeping the truth from the American public. MOM publishes the monthly newsletter *Taking Aim* and also makes available to the public documentary videos and weekly intelligence update audiotapes.

Northern Michigan Regional Militia (NMRM)
7578 Mission Rd.
Alanson, MI 49706
(616) 548-5878
fax: (616) 548-4867
e-mail: nolso@sunny.ncmc.cc.mi.us

NMRM's goal is to defend both America's and Michigan's constitutions. It works to ensure that all citizens, regardless of race, color, religion, sex, physical characteristics, or national origin, have the right and opportunity to due process of law as established and guaranteed by the Constitution of the United States. It publishes the *Northern Michigan Regional Militia Handbook*.

Rights in America
PO Box 38335
Colorado Springs, CO 80937
phone and fax: (719) 633-2740
internet: http://www.databahn.net/rights/

Rights in America is a monthly digest published for the purpose of offering continuing inquiry and commentary on the subject of rights in the American social, political, and legal arenas. *Rights in America* believes that in the quest for individual and group rights during recent decades, citizens have lost sight of other important attributes that made America great, including personal responsiblity; dedication to family, community, and nation; and shared commitment to the common good.

Second Amendment Foundation
12500 NE Tenth Pl.
Bellevue, WA 98005
(206) 454-7012
fax: (206) 451-3959

The foundation is dedicated to informing Americans about their Second Amendment right to keep and bear firearms. It believes that gun-control laws violate this right. The foundation, which neither opposes nor supports private militia groups, publishes the quarterly newsletters the *Second Amendment Reporter* and the *Gottlieb/Tartaro Report* and the magazines *Gun Week* and *Women and Guns*.

Southern Poverty Law Center
PO Box 2087
Montgomery, AL 36102
(334) 264-0286
fax: (334) 264-8891

The Southern Poverty Law Center litigates civil cases to protect the rights of poor people, particularly when those rights are threatened by white supremacist groups. The affiliated Klanwatch Project and Militia Task Force collect data on white supremacist groups and militias and promote the adoption and enforcement of antiparamilitary training laws. The center publishes numerous books and reports, including *False Patriots: The Threat of Antigovernment Extremists* and the monthly *Klanwatch Intelligence Report*.

Bibliography

Books

Tricia Andryszewski	*The Militia Movement in America: Before and After Oklahoma City*. Brookfield, CT: Millbrook, 1997.
David H. Bennett	*The Party of Fear: The American Far Right from Nativism to the Militia Movement*. New York: Vintage, 1995.
Morris Dees and James Corcoran	*Gathering Storm: America's Militia Network*. New York: HarperCollins, 1996.
Stephen P. Halbrook	*That Every Man Be Armed: The Evolution of a Constitutional Right*. Rev. ed. Oakland, CA: Independent Institute, 1994.
Thomas Halpern and Brian Levin	*The Limits of Dissent: The Constitutional Status of Armed Civilian Militias*. Northampton, MA: Alethia Press, 1996.
Neil A. Hamilton	*Militias in America*. Santa Barbara, CA: ABC-CLIO, 1996.
Jonathan Karl	*The Right to Bear Arms*. New York: HarperCollins, 1995.
Ian Koch	*The Militia Battle Manual*. El Dorado, AR: Delta Press, 1995.
Larry Pratt	*Safeguarding Liberty: The Constitutional Liberties and the Citizens' Militias*. Springfield, VA: Gun Owners of America, 1996.
Kenneth S. Stern	*A Force upon the Plain: The American Militia Movement and the Politics of Hate*. New York: Simon & Schuster, 1996.
Jess Walter	*Every Knee Shall Bow: The Truth and Tragedy of Ruby Ridge and the Randy Weaver Family*. New York: HarperCollins, 1995.

Periodicals

Chip Berlet and Holly Sklar	"Militias and Conspiracy Theories," interview with Chip Berlet and Holly Sklar, by David Barsamian, *Z Magazine*, September 1995.
Alan W. Bock	"Weekend Warriors," *National Review*, May 29, 1995.
Devin Burghart and Robert Crawford	"Vigilante Justice: Common Law Courts," *Covert Action Quarterly*, Summer 1996.
David Corn	"The New Minutemen," *Nation*, May 6, 1996.
Barbara Dority	"Is the Extremist Right Entirely Wrong?" *Humanist*, November/December 1995.
Peter Doskoch	"The Mind of the Militias," *Psychology Today*, July/August 1995.

Tod Ensign

"The Militia-Military Connection," *Covert Action Quarterly*, Summer 1995.

Thomas Halpern, David Rosenberg, and Irwin Suall

"Militia Movement: Prescription for Disaster," *USA Today*, January 1996.

Dennis Henigan

"Militias Misinterpret Constitution," *National Law Journal*, June 12, 1995.

Mark Jackson

"Stop the Blanket Indictments of Militia," *Law Enforcement Alliance of America Advocate*, Summer/Fall 1995. Available from LEAA, 7700 Leesburg Pike, Suite 421, Falls Church, VA 22043.

William F. Jasper

"More Pieces to the OKC Puzzle," *New American*, June 24, 1996. Available from PO Box 8040, Appleton, WI 54913-8040.

Klanwatch Intelligence Report

Entire issue on militias, June 1995. Available from Southern Poverty Law Center, 400 Washington Ave., Montgomery, AL 36104.

David Kopel

"The Federal Government Should Set a Better Example," *Vital Speeches of the Day*, March 1, 1996.

Serge F. Kovaleski

"The Montana Militia's Call to Arms," *Washington Post National Weekly Edition*, May 8–14, 1995.

Wade Lambert

"Militias Are Joining Jury-Power Activists to Fight Government," *Wall Street Journal*, May 25, 1995.

Joe Maxwell and Andrés Tapia

"Guns and Bibles," *Christianity Today*, June 19, 1995.

Scott McLemee

"Reading from Left to Right: Resources on Right-Wing Militias," *Independent Politics*, July/August 1995.

William Pierce

"There's a Conspiracy: There Are Groups in America Today Working to Abolish Our Constitutional Rights," *Free Speech*, January 1996. Available from PO Box 330, Hillsboro, WV 24946.

Lou Prato

"Militias: Rushing to Judgment," *World & I*, September 1995. Available from 3600 New York Ave. NE, Washington, DC 20002.

Dave Skinner

"In Defense of the Militia," *USA Today*, July 1996.

Kenneth S. Stern

"Militia Mania: A Growing Danger," *USA Today*, January 1996.

John M. Swomley

"Armed and Dangerous: The Threat of the 'Patriot Militias,'" *Humanist*, November/December 1995.

Jeffrey A. Tucker

"Who Are the Freemen?" *Chronicles*, July 1996. Available from PO Box 800, Mount Morris, IL 61054.

Randy Weaver

"He's a Rallying Cry of the Far Right but a Reluctant Symbol," interview with Randy Weaver, by Ken Fuson, *New York Times*, August 27, 1995.

Index